EASY PC

EASY PC

HOW TO USE YOUR FIRST COMPUTER

Dr Kenneth Mole

RIGHT WAY

Copyright notice

© Elliot Right Way Books MM

Conditions of sale

This book shall only be sold, lent, or hired, for profit, trade, or otherwise, in its original binding, except where special permission has been granted by the Publishers.

Whilst care is taken in selecting Authors who are authoritative in their subjects, it is emphasised that their books can reflect their knowledge only up to the time of writing. Information can be superseded and printers' errors can creep in. This book is sold, therefore, on the condition that neither Publisher nor Author can be held legally responsible for the consequences of any error or omission there may be.

Typeset in 11 on 13½ pt by Letterpart Ltd., Reigate, Surrey.

Printed and bound in Great Britain by Cox & Wyman Ltd., Reading, Berkshire.

The *Right Way* series is published by Elliot Right Way Books, Brighton Road, Lower Kingswood, Tadworth, Surrey, KT20 6TD, U.K. For information about our company and the other books we publish, visit our web site at www.right-way.co.uk

Contents

ACKNOWLEDGEMENTS

Acknowledgement is made to the following companies and products mentioned in this book, many of which are registered as trademarks:

Microsoft Corporation

Microsoft ® Windows 95

Microsoft ® Windows 98

Microsoft ® WordPad

Microsoft ® Paint

Microsoft ® Outlook Express

INTRODUCTION

'Easy' manuals for beginners, written by experts, are baffling because experts have forgotten what it was like to be beginners. It is true that computing is easy, but only when explained to a beginner by a beginner.

So I began writing this guide from the moment I first sat down to my first computer. In no time at all, you too will be word-processing, managing documents, drawing pictures, e-mailing and Web surfing with ease. There's a wonderful world out there!

The basic machinery you need is a PC (Personal Computer) equipped with Windows 95 or Windows 98, a printer, some **floppy disks** and loudspeakers. There is a screen (the **monitor**) and a keyboard for typing. There is a slot or drawer, also known as a drive window, where a **compact disc** (a CD or CD-ROM) fits when you press the button beneath it, and a smaller slot into which a floppy disk fits. Try them out for size. Older PCs may not have a CD slot. Newer ones may have a slot for DVDs (Digital Versatile Discs – super CD-ROMs which can produce movies and surround sound) or even a CD-R slot. The ROM of CD-ROM stands for Read Only Memory. The R of CD-R stands for Recorder because you can record or save on a CD in that slot, not just read it.

Many people with a 14 inch monitor wish they'd spent a little more on a larger one. A 17 inch one gives almost a 50% bigger screen area. I'm glad I splashed out and changed my 14 inch one for a 17 inch.

When your new PC arrives, someone knowledgeable must do the installation for you and give a basic demonstration of how it all works. However, $1\frac{1}{2}$ seconds after they've left the room, your mind will revert to a blind blank. At least ask your installer how to switch on and how to switch off. (If you forget how to switch off, read page 28.) Dealers busy installing their wares can't be expected to spare time teaching in detail: that's why you need this book.

Have a printer installed for you from the beginning, as fitting one can be daunting. For using the Internet or e-mail you need to have a telephone socket within easy reach. For faxing you need to have a fax driver installed, but, before you do, read Chapter 19 on faxing, as it doesn't suit everybody.

Words like *compact disc*, *monitor* or *scanner*, which may need further explanation, are found in the index at the end of this book. They are printed in **bold** type (unless they are sub-headings) and you can expect further explanation if you look them up in the index, and they stand out clearly when you turn from the index to the page to which the index refers.

MAKE A HABIT OF USING THE INDEX: IT'S YOUR BEST FRIEND!

Because one PC differs from another, what appears on your screen may differ slightly from what's described in this book – different colours for instance, or minor variations in procedure. Do not worry about minor differences.

Exercise 1

SINGLE-CLICKING

Switch on by pressing what is probably the largest button on the front of the PC. (You may need to switch on the monitor as well.) Your floppy disk slot should be empty. If it isn't, a message will appear on the screen saying something like non-system disk or disk error, so you're already in trouble, but you can get out of it. Remove the disk (by pressing the button near the floppy disk slot) and then press **any key** on your keyboard as, if you look carefully, your screen will tell you to do. After various unintelligible messages have come and gone, your screen stops changing. What it now shows is called your **Desktop**. It is what you now see on your monitor: a coloured background on which are scattered little pictures called Icons, each labelled underneath with a name.

Look for the name My Computer. We shall now change that name, not because it strikes some people as tacky, but because we shall learn a lot in the process of changing it.

The end of your mouse farthest away from you has two Buttons you can press, a right one and a left one. (Some have three Buttons, a middle one as well.) Get your mouse pointer to rest on the name **My Computer**, like this:

Now *press and release* the left mouse Button. That press and release action is called clicking. **My Computer** will become highlighted, changing colour:

Your colours may vary, but highlighting will be obvious. Left click again. The name box now incorporates a **cursor**, a vertical bar that blinks:

If you've had any difficulty so far, it's probably because the mouse moved when you clicked it. Cultivate a secure touch – don't jiggle as you click. It may stray because your hand is shaking with excitement or from old age. Many beginners' frustrations are due to wobbling. Perhaps children are computer naturals because they have small fingers.

A Summary of Exercise 1

Switch on. Put your mouse arrow on the name **My Computer**. Click to highlight it. Click again to make it blink. Type **the whole shebang**. Click on the Desktop to confirm. Click again on the Desktop to get it off duty, unhighlighted.

To reverse the process, you clicked **the whole shebang** to highlight it, making it ready for action, and clicked it again to make it blink. You typed **My Computer**, then clicked on the Desktop as confirmation and finished by clicking again on the Desktop to get **My Computer** unhighlighted, off duty. The Desktop is now back to where it started and you now know how to click.

If, at this point, you want to take a break for a cup of tea, have a quick look at page 28 for details of how to shut down the computer safely.

Exercise 2

DOUBLE-CLICKING

With the Desktop showing on your screen, point your mouse arrow onto the **My Computer** icon – the little image of a monitor and keyboard – and click. The icon and its name become highlighted, going from weak colours to strong ones, meaning, "We have been chosen for action". Click again and nothing happens. That's because in order to see what's represented by an icon you have to double-click, i.e. click it twice in very quick succession. This opens it up to show what it's the symbol for. Double-clicking takes practice. If you get it right, a window appears, called in its top left hand corner by the same name as the icon you double-clicked – in this case **My**

Computer. (To get rid of a window, to **close** it, click the ☒ in the top right hand corner.) If you've got the My Computer window in front of you click its ☒. Then practise opening the My Computer window again by double-clicking the My Computer icon or its name on the Desktop. You can double-click the icon or its name; it makes no difference. The name is tied to its icon like a luggage label. The difference is only important when you want to single-click on the label in order to change its name. Practise shutting the window by clicking the ☒ and opening it again.

If you find double-clicking difficult, there are two solutions. The first is to click just once and then press **Enter** ⬅ on the keyboard. That works in the same way as a double-click and is easier for beginners. The second solution is to alter the timing of the double-click. You may not need to do this, but the process of doing so is instructive. For this, click the Start Button ▓Start, seen on the left hand bottom corner of your screen. (If a message now appears saying, "What do you want your computer to do?" it means that your hand must have slipped on the mouse, moving the arrow from ▓Start to Shut Down, the command immediately above ▓Start. If this has happened, put your mouse arrow on No or on Cancel and click.)

When you put your mouse arrow on ▓Start, the words "Click here to begin" may appear, but you can ignore that. It's just your machine trying to be helpful. Click ▓Start and a **Menu** appears. This is usually on a pale grey background. (To get rid of a Menu, click anywhere except on the Menu itself or on an icon.)

Now move your mouse arrow, without clicking, upwards over the Menu, passing over Run, Help and Find ▸ until it has arrived over Settings ▸ which will turn

darker as you reach it. Move to the right across **Settings** ▸
in the direction of the little arrowhead ▸ which is telling you
that there is more information over there in that direction.
Sure enough, Control Panel, Printers and others appear on
the right. Move your mouse arrow horizontally out of
Settings to the right. You can now move it down or up
again to single out one of these. When the arrow is on
Control Panel, it becomes highlighted. That means it is
operational, on duty, at your service. Click it and it will
open. (On a Menu, a single-click selects an item.)

Among the two dozen or so items shown in that **Control
Panel** window – in alphabetical order – is one called
Mouse. To see what it is, put your ▯ on it and doubleclick.
If you have clicked correctly, an **egg-timer** ⧖ will momen-
tarily appear – a request that you should wait a moment.
(Instead of double-clicking, you can of course click just
once and press the **Enter** key on the keyboard.) This
double-click opens the **Mouse** item on the **Control Panel**
window to reveal what it stands for, the **Mouse Properties window**.

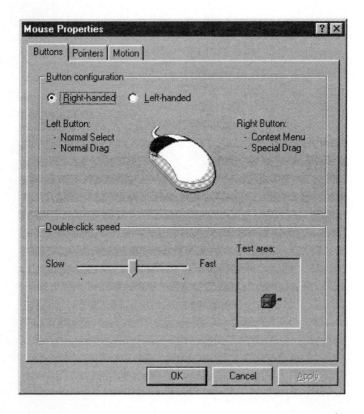

Put your ▷ over the slider between **Slow** and **Fast**, press the left clicker and, keeping it pressed down, move the mouse sideways. The slider will also move.

By doing this you can alter the double-click speed from **Fast** to **Slow**. Moving something in this way, by moving the mouse with a clicker pressed, is called **dragging**.

This fiddling with double-click speeds may seem a triviality, but by playing with the Mouse Properties window we can learn a lot about many other windows we shall come across. Note, for instance, the **question mark** at the top right hand corner of the Mouse Properties window. This appears on several windows. Click the ? and release the clicker. When you move your mouse the ? will now move as well. Move the ? to the **Test area**. Now click again. The answer to your question now appears – it should be something like this:

Provides a place for you to test the double-click speed of your mouse. If the jack-in-the-box emerges or disappears, your double-click was recognized.

(To get rid of a message, click elsewhere on the Mouse Properties window.) Move your mouse arrow into the test area and double-click. If you've got it right, the jack-in-the-box pops up. To put it back, double-click again. Try clicking the ? again and moving it to **Right-handed** and clicking it there. The answer it gives is:

Assumes that your left mouse button is the one you use most often. You generally click this button by using the index finger of your right hand.

The next few paragraphs are tricky, the only difficult ones in this whole book, but persevere. If you are left-handed and want to change your mouse so that you can use your left hand to work it, read what follows very carefully. If you don't want to make a change, it's worth reading all the same, because you'll learn something useful.

The dot in a white circle ⊙, which you can see next to **Right-handed** on the **Mouse Properties** window, marks an option which has been chosen. A circle without a dot in it ○, marks an **option** which has not been chosen. (A window with one black-dotted circle and other un-dotted ones is called a **dialogue box**.)

Try changing the **default** or pre-selected option, which is **Right-handed**, (pre-selected by your machine because most people are right-handed) by moving your mouse arrow to the **Left-handed** white circle and clicking that. Sure enough, the black dot now appears there, but you can't change to **Left-handed** yet because you have first to confirm your choice by clicking **Apply**. As you're still in **Right-handed** mode, it is an ordinary left-click that is required to accept the **Apply**. Only after the **Apply** is clicked is the left-handed mouse option working. Only then can you transfer the mouse to your left hand and use your left forefinger on the right mouse Button for ordinary clicking. To revert to the right-handed option, move your mouse arrow to the **Right-handed** white circle and click there. **Right-handed** is now marked with a ⊙, but won't be operational until **Apply** is clicked, and, as you are now in left-handed mode, you must use your right clicker to accept the **Apply**. All this is obvious to children and computers, who are more logical than grown-ups whose intuition can get them into terrible Windows frustration.

One moral of that treacherous paragraph is that much beginner's bewilderment is due to the machine being under orders which are not appreciated by its operator. Sometimes this is due to ignorance or forgetfulness, sometimes to a misplaced mouse or mistyped key. Occasionally a **gremlin** is the only possible explanation. For hints on getting out of trouble see STUCK! in the index.

Another moral is that you must be on the look-out for **OK, Apply** and similar suggestions, because you won't be able to progress unless you play your part by responding. You may, for instance, at various times be invited to click **Yes, No, OK, Apply, Cancel, Done, Close, Quit, Display, Exit** or whatever is offered. You're stuck until you respond.

There is another lesson here. The screen may often be full of stuff you can't or don't need to understand, but make a habit of glancing all over it. There may be something there that will save you hours of frustration, something as simple as clicking an **OK** you hadn't noticed.

Before we can get on to anything more serious, there is another lesson to be learnt from the Mouse Properties window. At the top you will see what are called **tabs**.

Many windows have them. This window has three or four of them, **Buttons**, **Pointers**, **Motion** and maybe **General** as well. Click each one in turn and glance at what is offered – mostly unimportant. The lesson here is that you must not try to digest everything that a window offers; you must learn to select only what you need.

Here is a summary of the steps you have taken so far in Exercise 2. Move to **Start**. Click. Move up to **Settings** ▸. Move horizontally to the right. Choose **Control Panel** and click. Choose **Mouse** and double-click. Drag the slider to **Slow** and confirm by clicking **OK**. The Mouse Properties window may close by itself, but if not click its ✖ to close it. Click ✖ on the Control Panel window to close that one also.

In short: ▓Start – **Settings** ▸ **Control Panel** – **Mouse** – **Slow** – **OK** – ✖ back to the Desktop.

Icons

With Windows, almost everything has a little **icon** plonked beside it, but you will find that you can safely look at the name of an item, not its icon. There were a good twenty icons on the Control Panel window you had open just now, but you chose **Mouse** because it was spelt that way, not because of its icon (a little picture of a computer mouse). Icons come into their own when sitting on little Buttons too small to have their names on. We meet Buttons in the next exercise.

Exercise 3

MANIPULATING WINDOWS

Whatever occupies your screen – be it your Desktop, a window or several windows – a bar will show, usually on the bottom edge.

This, recognisable by the oblong Start Button on its left, is the **taskbar**. (If it's not there, follow what is in the Index under taskbar not present.)

If you put your mouse arrow ⃗ over the taskbar and press and keep pressed the left clicker, you can drag the taskbar to any edge of the screen. It is usually at the bottom but some people like it at the top. Here are some other tricks:

1. Starting from the Desktop, double-click My Computer (or click it once to highlight it and press the Enter key). The My Computer window then appears:

🖳 **My Computer**   _ 🗗 ✕

At the right hand end of its titlebar are three little
Buttons. If the middle one is 🗗, as in the picture above,
put your ⌕ on it and click. The **My Computer** window will
shrink. This can be useful when you want to make room
for something else on your screen. (When you shrink a
window, the 🗗 Button changes to ◻.) If the middle one
is ◻, click it and the window expands to occupy the
whole screen. Clicking ◻ is called **maximising a window**.
When it's maximised, the middle of the three Buttons
changes back from ◻ to 🗗, ready for shrinking, in case
that's what you want.

Now click the left Button, ▄. The window becomes
minimised, collapsing to the taskbar, where it remains
represented by an oblong Button labelled with its icon and
its name, **My Computer**.

Minimising is a way of putting a window temporarily
out of the way. You will see that the buttons go in and out
when clicked:

🖳 My Computer   is out, 🖳 **My Computer**   is in.

By clicking on that **My Computer** Button on the taskbar
you can bring the **My Computer** window back to occupy
the screen. Then shrink it.

2. Put your mouse arrow ⌕ into the titlebar at the top of
the **My Computer** window and, holding down the clicker,
move the arrow about with your mouse. This is known as

dragging a window about. When you release the clicker, the window stays in its new position.

If you're stuck with a window with its titlebar missing, with no ✖ to click, click on any sliver of its titlebar at the top of the screen. You can then drag the window down or to the left for the ✖ to show up again.

3. Point your ⍓ carefully and accurately at any of the four edges of a shrunken window. Don't press the clicker until the ⍓ changes into a **double-headed arrow** ↕. You can then drag that edge in any direction, altering the size and shape of the window. You can do the same sort of thing if you land accurately on a corner.

Your next trick shows you how to manage several windows at a time. ✖ away any open windows so as to have a clear Desktop. Click ⊞Start. Move your ⍓ up to Settings and across to Control Panel and click. Make sure that the Control Panel window is shrunk (by pressing the ⊟, if available), then put your ⍓ into the titlebar of the Control Panel window and drag it to a lower part of the screen. Click ⊞Start again and go up to Settings again. This time go over to Printers and click and shrink that. Drag the window's titlebar down to the lower part of the screen, on top of the Control Panel window. Click ⊞Start a third time and go up to Find. Go across to Files or Folders and click that. Drag the Find: All Files window down, like the others, to make more room on your screen. You now have three windows open, Control Panel, Printers and Find: All Files. Each open window is represented by a Button on the taskbar:

A click on one of those taskbar Buttons jumps its window up to the front of the screen. Click on another Button and the window which that one represents will also open up, in front of the previous one. Try it. This is a useful manoeuvre for **switching from one window to another** when you're working on more than one window at the same time.

When you close a window by ✖ing it, its Button on the taskbar disappears. You can close a window represented on the taskbar by clicking its Button there and ✖ing it when it opens up. You can also close it by a **right-click on its Button on the taskbar** and choosing Close.

You can make the **taskbar thicken**, to give it more space for the name of the windows, by putting the mouse arrow over its upper edge, waiting for the ↕ to appear, and then dragging upwards, but it's good practice to keep your taskbar uncluttered.

4. You now have three windows open. Click a bit of window lurking behind others and that window will come to the front. Try clicking on each window in turn.

The taskbar, being only as wide as your screen, has to use **abbreviations** when it has to show on it more names of windows than it can spell out in full. It then gives a shortened version of the name followed by full stops . . . To see the full name of such an abbreviation, rest your ⌖ for a second on the abbreviated version and the full name will appear.

5. If you right-click, accurately, on a sliver of taskbar between two Buttons, a Menu appears with the command **Cascade Windows**. Click that and your three messy windows will arrange themselves neatly.

You can bring one of your choice to the front by clicking on a bit of it, or by clicking on its Button on the

taskbar, as I have done here with Find: All . . . Cascaded windows have a neat line of ✕s which are easy to click.

6. A right-click on the taskbar will offer **Minimize All Windows**. This is useful for revealing your **Desktop**. (Even better is the icon 🖼, present on some taskbars, a click on which will reveal your Desktop.) You can restore minimised windows by clicking them one by one on the taskbar or you can right-click on the taskbar again and click Undo Minimise All.

If the **taskbar has disappeared** below the bottom of the screen, put your ⬚ over the bottom of the screen until the double-headed arrow ↕ appears. This may take patience. Keeping the clicker pressed, drag upwards. When the taskbar is showing, clicking the 🏁Start Button can display the Start Menu in front of any windows that may be open.

Don't try to learn all of this exercise. Use the index and refer back to items printed in bold. Don't try to remember when to single-click (which is to *single* things out for attention) and when to double-click (which is to *open* things up). You will soon remember what comes in useful to you and forget the rest. You will, however, gradually come automatically to remember a few **right-clicks**. Some are listed in the Index.

Exercise 4

SHUTTING DOWN

After a few minutes, whatever is showing on screen may be replaced by an image called a **screen saver**. If your screen saver is in action and you want to restore your screen, jiggle the mouse.

To get rid of your screen saver, go **Start – Settings ▸ Control Panel – Display** – click the **Screen Saver** tab. In the **Screen Saver** box click on the ▼ to bring up a list of options, and scroll to find **None**. Select **None** and click **OK**. If you want to have fun with a personalised screen saver, click the **Screen Saver** tab and, instead of **None**, select, say, **Scrolling Marquee** if available. Click **Settings**. Choose a **Background color**. Type in, say, **Just don't PANIC, Geraldine**. Click **OK** on that window and **OK** again on the next window. ✖ away the Control Panel window, wait, and you'll see **Just don't PANIC, Geraldine** scrolling by. (Computers vary on the details of this procedure, so don't worry if it doesn't work first time for you.)

When you want to shut down your computer, you must check that all programs are shut. So empty your taskbar of any Buttons showing program names there by right-clicking and selecting **Close**. Then go to ![Start], on the left end of the *taskbar*, click, move up to **Shut Down**, the next item above it, and click that. In the **Shut Down Windows** window which then appears, click the circle **Shut down**, if empty, so as to turn it into one with a dot ⊙ and click **OK**.

When you switched on, your machine was first occupied in preparing itself, the screen finally settling down to the Desktop. If you switched off without giving it time to reverse this preparation, not only might you lose work you had done, but the machine would be left in a half-baked state, so that the next time you switched on you would have to wait while this muddle was sorted out. That's why you are finally told, when **Shut Down** is clicked, **It's now safe to turn off your computer**, which you do by pressing the same button which you used to turn it on. (Some machines, however, turn themselves off.)

When should you switch off your machine? The experts don't agree about that. Some people don't turn their computers off, ever. They say that keeping the temperature constant is a Good Thing, as it is for storing wine, and that constant wear and tear from switching on and off is a Bad Thing. Other people say it is a Bad Thing to leave it on all the time because the monitor wears and the computer's components get overheated. I turn mine off at night, if only to remove that telltale gleam from the curtains. As a further burglar precaution I also switch off when leaving the house.

Exercise 5

CHOOSING PROGRAMS

Switch on. Click ▓Start on the taskbar. Go up to **Pro-grams ▸**. Note the little arrowhead ▸ on the right of **Programs**. Wait half a second and the names of programs appear where the arrow is pointing to. To get rid of this **Start** Menu, click anywhere else on the screen and you're back to the Desktop. Begin again with ▓Start, go up again to **Programs ▸**. (To choose an item on a Menu, single it out with a single-click.) After waiting that half second, a vast Menu of programs appears on the right, where the arrowhead is pointing. There's an extremely wide choice because many of them have arrowheads themselves, point-ing to even more programs. If your ▹ rests on an item with an arrowhead ▸, the names of the programs to which it is pointing will appear. You can then click on the program of your choice. Many of these you will never use, so don't be dismayed because there are so many of them.

When the programs to which **Programs ▸** is pointing appear, go up to the top, to **Accessories ▸**. Sure enough, after half a second, what that arrowhead is pointing to appears. Go horizontally to this further Menu of programs. One choice is **Games** ▸. Go horizontally to the selection of games offered, not because it's playtime but because we'll learn a lot by doing so. Click **Solitaire**, the card game many of us know as Patience.

You play Solitaire by **dragging and dropping** the cards about. To drag and drop something, point on it with your mouse arrow, press down the left clicker and, keeping it pressed, move the mouse about. The object that you pointed at will move also. That's the *dragging* action. When it is where you want it, release the clicker. That's the *dropping* action. To practise dragging and dropping, try moving a few cards about in this way. If they don't want to stay where you put them, that's only because the rules of the game say they can't.

To read those rules, point to the word Help, which shows just beneath the window's title, Solitaire, and click. Go down to Help Topics, click that and click a topic, display it and read all about the game. Many windows

have a Help Menu, the topics dealt with being relevant to
the subject of that particular window (see page 86 for
more about Help).

You can now choose to play Solitaire, to ☒ the window
away, to shrink it, to minimise it down to the taskbar, or
to forget about it until the time comes to switch off, when
you must make sure the window is closed.

This time, forget about it and profit from the way you
can leave stuff on your screen and press on regardless.
This is thanks to the constant availability of the Start
Button on the taskbar for starting something else and
from the fact that the most recently opened window
always shows up in front of earlier ones. The limitation
is that an overburdened computer slows down.

So press 🏁Start and go again to Programs ▸ Accessories ▸ Games. This time click Hearts. A window called
The Microsoft Hearts Network shows. I see on my
version of this window that my nephew has been there
before me and typed in his name, so I just click OK so as
to press on. This opens a window full of playing cards.
Click Help – Help Topics and then click on Playing
Hearts. Ignore the details of To Play Hearts in the right
hand pane of the window which now appears, but just
notice that there is more in this window than can be
contained in one screen's worth. The problem is over-
come by a **scroll bar**. The Hearts Help window has a
vertical scroll bar on its right edge. At its bottom is an
arrowhead ▾ pointing downwards and at its top is one
pointing upwards ▴. Between the two is a **slider** which
you can click and drag up or down like a lift in a
lift-shaft. When a window contains a document even 100
or more pages long, by dragging the slider you can move
over all of it with fantastic speed. One click on an

arrowhead moves you up or down a line. A click just above or below the slider scrolls a whole screen's length.

Some windows provide a horizontal scroll bar at the bottom, with ◄ and ► for clicking and a slider for dragging, so as to reveal what's on either side of the screen to right or left.

When a window has two panes, you can enlarge one pane at the expense of the other by resting your ▷ on the interface between the two and waiting for it to change to a double arrow ◄► and then dragging sideways.

Now clear your screen of windows by clicking any ✖ so as to get back to the Desktop ready for the next exercise. Or, you can get the same result by clearing your taskbar with a right-click on any Button there and clicking Close.

Exercise 6

WORD-PROCESSING

6.i WordPad

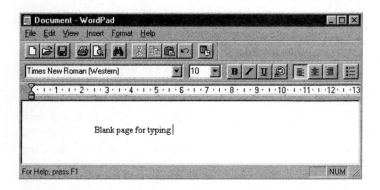

On a typewriter, what you type is often called a 'document'. In a word-processing program on your computer you can also type a **document**, but, in computerspeak, it is usually called a File.

The word '**File**' is computer jargon, often interchangeable with the word 'document'. In ordinary speech, a File is a box or folder for holding a number of individual items stored under the same name. In computerspeak, however, a File may be not a *collection* of items stored under one name, but just one *single* item. And, furthermore, a File may be words on a page, a blank page, a chapter of a book, a whole book, a picture, a set of instructions, a recording of music or a mixture of any such items.

The computerspeak name for a *collection* of Files is a **Folder**. Another name for a Folder is a **Directory**. You'll soon get used to this jargon and find yourself speaking it like a native.

We shall now type a document or, in other words, create a File. To do this we first have to find somewhere in which to type it. Your computer provides this, a program designed for this purpose, a blank page called WordPad.

This is the name of the most basic word-processing program offered by Windows. It has its weaknesses – it can type only in **single-spacing** and it can't count words or check spelling – so you may want to add to your PC a better system by buying some extra software. There are several on the market, but they may offer so much more that they will be just more confusing as well. So, unless you are already familiar enough with word-processing not to be confused, it will pay for you to follow the four exercises offered here. You may find them rudimentary because word-processors, being descendants of the iron age typewriter, all work on the same principles. Once you've mastered WordPad, a more sophisticated system will be much easier to manage.

To open the program **WordPad**, go ▓Start – Programs ▶ Accessories ▶ and look for WordPad. Click that. On your screen is now a window called Document – WordPad, a blank page for you to type on.

Whatever your interest in computers, you will need the basic skills of word-processing, if only just to type the name of a File. Trial and error will teach you much, but follow the few tips given here.

The first essential is to get acquainted with the signs and symbols showing in the Document – WordPad window.

At the top of the window is the **Titlebar** with the name Document – WordPad appearing in light-coloured characters on a dark-coloured bar, as a title does in all windows. At the right-hand end of the titlebar are our friends the three little Buttons for maximising, shrinking and closing.

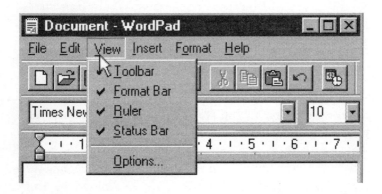

Below the Titlebar is the **Menu bar**. Menus vary from window to window. This one offers File, Edit, View, Insert, Format and Help. Click the word File and briefly cast your eye down the Menu which appears. Click Edit to glance at that Menu and then move over to View. (Note those underlined letters, such as the V in View. They refer to a method of choosing items on a Menu by pressing keys on the keyboard, a pre-mouse technique.) On the View

Menu are listed Toolbar, Format Bar, Ruler and Status Bar, each preceded by a **tick** ✔ (or **check mark**, as the Americans call it). Note that Menu options are specific to the windows in which they appear.

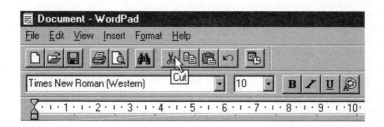

Next below the Menu bar is *usually* the **Toolbar**, recognisable by its display of a Button with the tool ✂ on it, also known as cut. If the Toolbar isn't showing, click open the View Menu and, if Toolbar isn't ticked there, click on it. That will produce both a tick on the Menu and the appearance on screen of the Toolbar. If, on the View Menu, there is a ✔ opposite Toolbar and you click it, the tick will disappear from the Menu and the Toolbar will disappear from view. (This means you can see more of what you are typing.)

The Toolbar presents a row of Buttons, each one identified by an icon. Icons come into their own here, because small Buttons have no room to display their names. These names you can see if you rest your ▷ over a Button. After a moment it will announce its function. Just for fun, click ▦, the Button at the extreme right, the one which calls itself **Date/Time**. Choose a style from the varieties you're offered and click OK. The date will now appear in your document. Delete it by pressing the **backspace key**, the one with a left-pointing arrow ←——, a key seen to the immediate left of the Insert key. If you put your ⍾ on the Toolbar in a space between Buttons, you can move it about by dragging.

The next line down is *usually* the **Format bar**. It can also be moved about by dragging. The oblong box on its left shows the name of the font (style of print or type face) currently operating. The box with a number in it refers to the size of print. The Buttons on the right, beginning with **B** for bold, also affect the form of what you type. Like all Buttons, those on the format bar can be pressed or released. **B** becomes **B** when pressed once, and **B** when pressed again. This clicking and re-clicking is called **toggling**. Pass your ⍾ along this bar, slowly, so as to give the icons time to announce their functions.

The line below is *usually* the **ruler**, and this can also be turned on or off by ticking/unticking on the View Menu.

When you've finished with the WordPad window, click its ✖. Then, when you're asked whether or not you want to save changes, click No.

Exercise 6

WORD-PROCESSING

6.ii Starting to Type

Start this exercise with WordPad. (**Start** – Programs ▶ Accessories ▶ WordPad.)

Move your mouse all over the WordPad window which appears. As you do, you'll see the **mouse pointer** Ι. Move it around with your mouse and you will see that it takes this shape when in a part of the screen on which you can type, but reverts to the second mark, your old friend the **mouse arrow** ↖, when there is something to be pointed at, such as an icon or a Button. Another mark you'll see is a blinking vertical line called the **Cursor**, |. Once you begin typing, it never stops blinking but waits for another character to be typed. As you type, the characters land on the space occupied by the Cursor, and the Cursor moves one space to the right to make room for the next character.

Examine your keyboard and look for familiar-looking

typewriter keys. Some will be strange. Try them out to see what they do. The group on the right of the keyboard with numbers on them is for doing sums. We'll come to that later. You can also ignore, for the moment, the F keys at the top. They are mostly a hangover from the days before the invention of the mouse, when everything was control-led from the keyboard. Almost everything can still be controlled from the keyboard, but the mouse, which began as a convenience, can still be a necessity.

Now type something, at least two paragraphs of it. Note that what you type appears where the Cursor is, not where the mouse pointer] happens to be. To **get the Cursor where you want it to be** (within the text you have typed), put the mouse pointer] at the chosen spot and click. The blinking Cursor will follow. You may find, until you get used to it, that you try to type where the pointer is, not where the Cursor is, because you've forgotten to move the Cursor to where you want to type.

To move the pointer across the page by large amounts, moving it by moving the mouse and clicking where you want to anchor it is fine, but for small jumps, such as between letters, you may find that the four **arrow keys on the keyboard** (←↓↑→) are easier to control.

The key **Home** jumps the Cursor to the beginning of a line, the key **End** jumps it to the end. If you hold down the key Ctrl (Control) at the same time as the Home or End keys, the Cursor goes to the beginning or end of the whole document. In order to produce capital letters, as well as the symbols such as ! @ £ % and so on which appear at the top of the number and symbol keys, press the **shift key** ⇧ at the same time as pressing the relevant key.

If, when using any word-processing program, you find that pressing the **pound sign £** produces #, and pressing @

produces ", your keyboard is thinking in **American English**. To change to British English, go Start – Settings ▶ Control Panel – Keyboard – Language. Click English (British) and Set as Default. Click OK. (You may be asked to insert your Windows 95 or 98 CD before you are able to do this.) If you now shut down your computer, the next time you switch on, your keyboard will think in British English.

If you've typed an incorrect letter, press the **backspace** ◄— **key**. This deletes what's immediately to the left of the Cursor. The key called **Delete** deletes all sorts of things, but, when you're typing, it deletes what lies immediately to the right of the Cursor.

Unlike the behaviour of an iron-age typewriter, when letters typed by a word-processor reach the end of a line they automatically go down to the line below, a process called **wordwrapping**. Pressing the **Enter key** interrupts this automatic process when you decide, for instance, to start a new paragraph. Pressing Enter puts you down at once to the start of the next line below. (To **reverse such an Enter**, press the backspace key.) If, at the beginning of a new paragraph, you want to start a few spaces in, first press the **Tab key**, the key with two opposite facing arrows on it ⇄, found just above the Caps Lock key at the left of the keyboard. It may be no longer fashionable to indent paragraphs, but many people prefer to do so.

The **Caps Lock key** controls whether you type in **UPPER CASE** (capitals) or lower case. Press it once to go on and once again to go off (toggling it on and off). It can be maddening when you forget Caps Lock is on, but on some keyboards there is a warning light (seen on the keyboard top right), telling you that Caps Lock is operating. Not all word-processors are clever enough to change to lower case something you've already typed in upper case letters.

If you press the **Insert key**, and put the Cursor immediately to the left of a letter already typed, what you now type will replace that letter. This is unnerving when you've pressed Insert by mistake, especially as the space bar now acts like the Delete key, deleting what's to the right. Press the Insert key again to get out of trouble.

Note the **Page Up** and **Page Down** (Pg Up and Pg Dn) keys at the right of the keyboard. These can help you to move up and down a long document, rather than using the arrow keys (which are slower) or the mouse and scroll bar (which can be unreliable).

Finish this exercise by clicking the ☒ in the top right hand corner of screen. You will then be asked whether or not you want to save changes. Click No.

Exercise 6

WORD-PROCESSING

6.iii Highlighting

You need WordPad again for this exercise. (▓Start –
Programs ▶ **Accessories** ▶ **WordPad**). Type a few sen-
tences so as to produce some text on which to practise.

If you want to alter the appearance of what you have
typed you must first pick out the bit you want to change by
highlighting it. Highlighting is also known as selecting. The
word highlighted is highlighted, dark letters on a light
background changed to light letters on a dark background.

There are several ways of doing this. One is by using
the mouse pointer, Ɪ. To **highlight a single word**, move the
mouse pointer over it and double-click. To **highlight a
chunk of text**, put the pointer at one end of it and hold
down the clicker while dragging in any direction, sideways or up and down. You can achieve the same effect
from the keyboard by keeping the shift key ⇧ pressed
while moving the cursor about with the arrows keys or

pressing the Home or End keys. Rather than use the wobbly mouse pointer to **highlight a single letter**, you may prefer to use the keyboard: press at the same time the shift key and an arrow key, either ← or → according to whether the mouse pointer is on to the right or the left of the character, so as to highlight just that letter. Only one word or whole section can be highlighted in one go – there cannot be unhighlighted chunks of text between highlighted words or sections. To **highlight a whole document**, either put your mouse pointer at the top left of the page and drag it to bottom right, or choose **Select All** from the Edit Menu. To **remove highlighting**, one click anywhere other than the highlighted section will do this. To delete what it is that you've highlighted, press **Delete**.

If you want to underline what you have typed, highlight it and click the <u>U</u> Button on the format bar. What you have highlighted then becomes underlined. To remove underlining, highlight what's underlined, click the <u>U</u> Button again and then click anywhere else. By toggling on the **B** / <u>U</u> Buttons you can make type **bold**, put it in *italics*, <u>underline</u> it or revert to un-bold, un-italicised or un-underlined. You can have the **B** / <u>U</u> Buttons all pressed down *<u>at the same time</u>*.

Besides using the Delete key, you can also remove what you've highlighted by clicking the **scissors Button** ✂, seen up there in the Toolbar. Try this out. Highlight something and cut it out with the scissors. It vanishes, but hasn't gone forever, because up there, three Buttons to the right of the scissors Button on the Toolbar, is the "Woops, sorry" Button, ↰. (If you rest your arrow on it and wait for half a second, you'll see that its name is **Undo**, short for Undo last command.) Click this and what you've just cut out will reappear. This is an icon to be blessed, because it's so easy to make a mistake.

To repeat, to remove highlighting, click anywhere. To delete what's highlighted, click ✂ or press the **Delete** key. Regretted actions are reversible by ↶ **Undo**.

Cut, Copy and Paste ✂ 🗐 📋
Scissors do more than just cut out what's highlighted; they *remember* what has been cut. Having cut a single letter, a word, a sentence or a whole File, you can then paste 📋 what you've cut out anywhere you like, as many times as you like, and even into a different document, such as an E-mail letter or Address Book. To choose where you want it to be pasted, mark the place you want to put it (called the **insertion point**) by putting the Cursor there. Then click on **Paste** 📋 and the job's done.

If an item is *dimmed* out, that means there is nothing for it to do. Paste, for instance, on the **Edit** Menu or ✂, the scissors icon on the Toolbar, only work if something has been highlighted to be pasted or to be cut.

Now rest your arrow on the Button 🗐 between **Cut** and **Paste**. Its name, Copy, will soon appear. Highlight some text, click Copy, and nothing much seems to happen apart from the highlighting. Your machine has copied what you have just highlighted and will paste it wherever you choose an insertion point by putting the Cursor there and clicking 📋 **Paste**. Once something is copied, you can swan all around your computer before going to where you want to paste it. And you can paste the same stuff over and over. But beware, anything awaiting pasting will be replaced by anything that's cut or copied afterwards. The earlier version, if cut out without being copied, will be forgotten, lost for ever, because only one bit of highlighting can be memorised at a time.

By clicking on the Edit Menu or on the Toolbar Buttons,
you can Cut, Copy and Paste from one document to
another and from one part of a document to another part of
the same document. You can also **drag text** from one part
of a document to another part. Highlight a word or some
text and click elsewhere and that will abolish the highlighting, but if you keep the mouse Button pressed you can drag
what's highlighted to another position on the page. If you
keep the Ctrl key pressed while doing this, the action won't
just move what's highlighted but will leave the original
intact where it was, making a copy of it elsewhere.

Mouse Versus Keyboard
Apart from typing on the **keyboard** and using keys like
Delete, shift and the arrow keys, many of the manoeuvres
of this exercise have been done with the mouse alone. All
of it, however, can be done direct from the keyboard, and,
while you are engaged in typing, this may be more conven-
ient than stopping to handle the mouse. Windows has
many ways of doing the same thing and keyboard meth-
ods have survived alongside the introduction of mouse
control.

If you highlighted something for underlining and
absentmindedly pressed the Delete key, you could use the
mouse to click ↶, the Undo Button, and rescue it. But
you could also order Undo from the keyboard. By holding
down the Alt key and then pressing E (E for Edit), the Edit
Menu appears. You can select any of the options on this
Menu by either clicking on it or using the arrows keys to
move the highlighting up and down. An item on this
Menu is Undo Ctrl+Z, meaning that pressing the keys Ctrl
and Z together gives the same command as clicking the
Undo Button (but you cannot do this while the Edit menu

is opened up). The keyboard shortcut for Cut on the keyboard is Ctrl + X, as you will see on the drop down Edit Menu. Copy, on the keyboard is Ctrl + C and Paste is Ctrl + V. Do what suits you best, probably a combination of mouse and keyboard.

In many word-processing programs you can highlight a whole line by clicking at its extreme left, in the margin. This means that if you use the mouse pointer to get the Cursor to the beginning of a line, it's very easy to go too far and stray into the margin and click there. If you do that, you'll highlight the line. If you don't want to high-light a line but just go to its beginning, it's better to send the Cursor there by pressing Home, rather than using the mouse pointer.

Finish this exercise by clicking the ✖ in the top right hand corner of the screen. You will then be asked whether or not you want to save changes. Click No.

Exercise 6

WORD-PROCESSING

6.iv Further Refinements

Once again, open WordPad. (**⊞Start** – Programs ▸ Accessories ▸ WordPad.)

Changing Fonts
Type in the WordPad window the sentence 'The quick brown fox jumps over the lazy dog'. It will appear on your screen in the default font, probably one called **Times New Roman**.

To choose a different **font** for that sentence, first highlight it and then click the little arrow **▼** in the left box of the format bar. When you scroll to a font listed there and click it, the quick brown fox sentence will appear in that font. If you scroll to a font called **Arial**, click that. What then appears is **The quick brown fox jumps over the lazy dog**. Different computers have different fonts on them, but somewhere amongst your list of fonts you may find some which produce symbols in the place of letters. If you chose the font **Botanical**, you will see ❀✿❁❃ ❄❅❆❇ ❈❉❊❋ ✢✣✤✥ ❀✿❁❃ ❄❅❆❇ ❈❉❊❋ ✢✣✤✥. The fourth group of symbols, ✢✣✤✥, was produced by typing the letters f, o and x, so if you wanted to produce the symbol ✢, you'd choose **Botanical** as your font and type f on the keyboard. Thus, that sentence about the fox and the dog, famous for containing all the letters of the alphabet, comes in useful when wondering how to type a symbol like ✢ which has no obvious relation to the keyboard. If you haven't got **Botanical**, try **Wingdings**. You can choose a font before typing text or you can highlight text and then choose what font you want for it.

Changing Point Size
The size of type is measured in points, one point being one 72nd of an inch. To change **point** size, highlight what you want to change, say the character ✢. (You will remember that, to highlight a single character, you put the mouse pointer immediately to its right or to its left and, with the shift key ⇧ pressed, move over the character by using the arrow keys.) Now click the little down arrow ▾ in the box with a number in it. This number refers to point size. (The box is seen on the Toolbar between the font name box and **B** *I* U .) Scroll to a number, say 18, to choose a different point size. The character ✢ will now become larger. As with fonts, and as with **B** *I* U , you can choose what you want before typing text or you can highlight text and then change it.

Viewing Fonts
There are two ways:

1. ▄Start – Settings ▸ Control Panel ▸ Fonts. Double-
   click on any font listed there and the whole range of
   characters in that font is displayed.
2. In the Wordpad window, click the Format Menu and
   choose Font . . . You are now offered just a sample
   of each font (and also a choice of size.) Whatever you
   choose and confirm by clicking on OK will operate
   anew when you start typing or will change what you
   have highlighted.

Keep your wits about you when changing font size or
type. A change can alter how much text will appear on
a printed page. Some fonts take up less room than
others.

Margins
To control **margins** on a whole page, choose Page Setup
on the File Menu of the WordPad window. The margins
are demonstrated on a small model of the page showing at
the top of the Page Setup window.

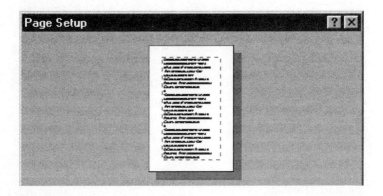

Type in the required measurements in the relevant boxes, not forgetting to click OK. (When **form-filling**, that is to say going from one box to another in a window, you can jump from box to box by pressing the Tab key.)

You may find that setting new margins, though showing on the ruler, has no effect on what you type. If so, you may be victim of the command No wrap, or **Wrap to window**. These commands can be reversed by choosing Options on the View Menu and clicking the Text tab in the Options window. Choose **Wrap to ruler** (not forgetting the OK) and your new margins will now behave. Note that altering the margins of a document will also alter how the page appears when printed.

This is an example of a frustrating situation where one command has been overruled by another somewhere in the system. If the Page Up, Page Down, Ctrl+Home and Ctrl+End keys don't work, it may be because a command window is open. A click anywhere is often the cure. If the wrong document appears, just ✖ it away; maybe some other File is waiting to be saved. Another example: your typing refuses to start on the left of the page. Perhaps there is a tab on your ruler (see page 52) or perhaps **Alignment Right** ▤ has been selected. It often helps to go back to the Desktop or even 🏁Start – Shut down and switch on again.

First Aid When Stuck

   1.   Press the space bar once. Try a left click. Try a right click. Try Esc (escape), the top left-hand key on the keyboard, though it's never worked for me.

2. Repeat what you had been trying to do. You may have pressed the wrong key or clicked the wrong icon.

3. Look at your screen; there may be an instruction there, such as **press any key**, or there may be an unchecked **Yes, No, OK, Cancel, Done, Close, Quit, Display** or **Exit** or **Apply**.

4. Is an unwanted command operating? See if any Button is pressed in or highlighted on the Toolbar or format bar, such as **Align right** or **Center**.

5. Note that when you want to reverse an action, toggling may work rather than **Undo**. Note also that you can often get rid of something stuck on your screen by calling up something else.

6. Remember that Menus, such as **View** or **Edit**, refer only to the window in which they appear. Menus in a window that lists the *names* of Files, for instance, differ from those in a window which shows the *contents* of a particular File.

There are more remedies listed in the index under stuck.

Tabs

(The same word '**tabs**' as on page 21 but used here in a different sense.) You can alter the margins of a line or a paragraph by dragging the **blobs on the ruler**. The blob on the left has an upper and a lower part. The upper part controls the first line of a paragraph, the lower part the rest of the paragraph.

To set the tabs, click on the ruler where you want to set them. A mark like ∟ will appear. You can drag a tab in either direction. It will operate when you press the Tab key ⇄. To get rid of a tab, drag it off the ruler. You can also click the Format Menu, choose Tabs and click Clear All and OK.

Find

This command is used for **finding a word in a document**. To practise this, type on the WordPad window a few lines of writing which contain the word bath. To find the word bath, click the find Button (▲ or something similar) on the Toolbar or click Find in the Edit Menu, so as to open the Find window. Accept the invitation of the blinking Cursor and type, in the Find what: box, the word bath. Then click Find Next. The word bath becomes highlighted, even if it's on page 100. Now ✕ away the Find window.

Here's another refinement. Add another word Bath, to the document, this time spelt with a capital B. Click open the Find window. Click the ? and move the mouse to rest the ? on **Match case** and click. The answer goes something like this:

Finds only text that has the same pattern of uppercase and lowercase characters as the text you specified in **Find what**.

Click away the answer and click a tick against Match case. In the Find what box delete the word bath and type Bath with a capital B. Now, when you click Find Next, the word bath won't be found but the word Bath will be.

You can also replace one word, wherever it occurs, with another. To try this, choose **Replace** on the Edit Menu and type in your desired replacement, say Bristol. Click Replace All and each word Bath in the document will be changed to the word Bristol. ☒ away the Find window and click anywhere to remove the highlighting.

Bullet Points
▤ the Button on the extreme right of the format bar, when clicked, starts a paragraph with a **bullet point** ✦. To cancel a bullet, don't try to Delete it but remember that toggling is the way to reverse the action of a Button. Undo won't pull the Button ▤ out, clicking the Button will.

Making a Letterhead
This can be done with a manoeuvre called **Scrap** (this works with WordPad, not on all word-processors). You can make several scraps and drag them into a Folder (see page 60 for making a Folder) which can then act as a clipboard containing more than one item waiting to be copied, unlike the one-item-at-a-time-only and invisible **clipboard** which can be loaded by Cut or Copy.

Highlight and Delete anything you've typed so as to clear the page, and type a letterhead using the alignment, point and font of your choice, say

```
             DR.  BARKING-MADDE
               THE  DOGHOUSE
               HOUNDSDITCH
                  BERKS
```

To change the **alignment** in WordPad, use the buttons towards the right of the Toolbar. To change to alignment left press ▦, to change to centred alignment (as above) press ▦, and to change to alignment right press ▦.

You could also, if you have a colour printer, **highlight for colour printing** any part of it and choose a colour from the color icon 🖉 on the format bar.

Now reduce with 🗗 the size of the Wordpad window so as to reveal a bit of Desktop. Highlight what you have typed, put the mouse pointer over the highlighting and drag what you've highlighted onto the Desktop. An icon appears on the Desktop labelled *WordPad Document Scrap 'Dr. Barking-Ma . . .'* Change that name to something simpler, say Letterhead (see page 11 to remind you how to change the name of an icon).

Letterhead remains on your Desktop ready for future use, because, when you next open WordPad to write a letter, you can reduce it so as to reveal the bit of Desktop which shows Letterhead on it and drag Letterhead on to your new letter. There, ready typed, will be your letterhead in whatever colours or style you had chosen.

You can have **today's date** typed in automatically by clicking Date and Time on the Insert Menu (or the Date/Time Button at the right end of the Toolbar 🗓) and OK-ing the style you want.

Finish this exercise by clicking the ✖ in the top right hand corner of the screen. Click No when you're asked whether or not you want to save changes.

Exercise 7

MAKING FILES AND FOLDERS

Saving

If you have any experience at all of word-processing, you will have learned, the hard way, that your work can disappear in a flash. Forever. This can happen if there's a power cut or if someone in the kitchen switches on a faulty gadget. The reason is that what you type is memorised only temporarily by your machine. If it's not permanently recorded – saved – before electricity is next cut off, it's gone.

People don't just go white after power cuts: they jump out of skyscraper windows. And then there's the **illegal operation**. Sometimes a window appears accusing me of having performed one. I am forced to click Close to shut that shameful window, but in doing so I lose any changes I have made since I last saved. This is particularly cruel because I have no notion of what I have done wrong.

One reason why beginners with Windows get confused is that there are so many ways of doing the same thing. Saving a document is a good example. You could click

File, to reveal the Menu, and then click the **Save** which appears there and that would take the document out of temporary memory. Or you could, as suggested on that Menu, press **Ctrl+S** on your keyboard. Or, yet another way, you could click the third Button from the left along the Toolbar, 🖫, which is also **Save**. I myself prefer to open the File Menu with my mouse and click anywhere on the long bar **Save**, rather than click on the 🖫 Button, simply because the Button is a bit insignificant for me to aim at.

When should you save? Being twice-shy I do it several times a page, any time I leave the room, and whenever I feel I owe it to posterity to preserve some thought of genius. This may be unnecessary; your machine will remind you at every opportunity not to forget to save. But I am terrified of the accusation of illegal operations and my electricity comes along wires supported by ancient wooden poles. Some word-processing **software** can save Files automatically, at chosen intervals.

It is still possible to lose stuff even if power cuts and illegal operations are avoided. We've seen that if you cut out some text and copy another lot before pasting it in, the first lot is lost to limbo. Another hazard is that a text window, opened as usual by double-clicking its icon+name, may, for no apparent reason, suddenly close back to the icon+name, losing everything on it. "The best-laid schemes o'mice an' men gang aft a-gley", especially o'mice.

Save As

If you have just typed a document – made a File – and clicked its ☒, your caring machine will want to make sure you really want to lose it, and so you will be asked **Save** changes to document? Yes, No or Cancel. Click No and it will disappear, but if you want to save it, what do you do? Let's type a new document and find out.

Open WordPad (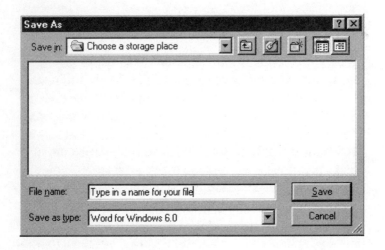 Start – Programs ▸ Accessories ▸ WordPad) and type Summer, sea, sand and sun. This is a five-word File. In computerspeak, a File consists of **data**, plural of the Latin word datum. If these data are not to be lost, they must be saved. Drop down the File Menu and click the Save As bar (or click the 💾 Button or save it some other way.)

You'll now see, blinking, a request for a **File name**. (If there's nothing blinking, get the Cursor into the File name box, if necessary clearing out, by means of the backspace key, anything already there. Type in a name for your document, say Bermuda. Near where you typed Bermuda there's a Button called Save. Don't click it yet, because you've still to decide *where* to store your document. Decide this by selecting something from the choice presented by clicking the ▼ Button in the **Save in box**. Click 🖴 [C:]. That action decides that your File will be stored in the huge filing cabinet called C (introduced in the next exercise). Having chosen a name and a place, you can now click Save.

Your document reappears, its name now changed from Document – WordPad, to Bermuda – WordPad, safe!

You *could* now remove it from the screen by ✖ing WordPad to get back to the Desktop before starting on your second document, but you don't *have* to clear the screen before opening another window. Go again to 🏁Start – Programs ▸ Accessories ▸ and when you click WordPad, Bermuda just gets covered up behind the new Document – WordPad window. (The most recently opened window is always in front.) In your new window, type the words Winter, ski, snow and sun. Click the File Menu and choose Save as (or click the save Button.) In the Save As window, select 🖴 [C:] again for the Save in box, and type Austria in the File name box. Now that you've chosen a name for your File and a place to store it in, click the Save Button. Your document reappears in the WordPad window, now entitled Austria – WordPad, safe! Click its ✖ to reveal the File Bermuda lurking behind it. Click Bermuda's ✖ and you're back to the Desktop.

Now let's check that your two Files are safely stored in C. Double-click My Computer and then 🖴 [C:] on the My Computer window. Sure enough, there, in the C window, Bermuda and Austria are listed. (You may have to scroll to the right to see where they are.)

Let's make a Folder called Holidays and put the Files Austria and Bermuda into it. Our C window is open, and

that's the filing cabinet where we want to store this
Folder. Right-click any empty space in this window and
choose **New** from the Menu that appears and then **Folder**.
A yellow Folder appears:

Type **Holidays** in the blinking name space and click (or
press the **Enter** key) to confirm.

To put the File **Bermuda** in this **Holidays** Folder, drag
it towards the Folder until **Holidays** becomes highlighted. Then release the clicker and the job's done. Do
the same with **Austria**. You can leave that **C** window
open while going to start for the third File we propose to
create.

For this, go ▓Start – Programs ▸ Accessories ▸ and,
instead of WordPad, this time click **Paint**. Study this
window. Have a look at what the Buttons on the left of
the Paint window do by resting your arrow on them one
by one. (These Buttons make up the Toolbox. This
behaves like the Toolbar in that, if it's not showing, a click
against Toolbox in the **View** Menu to tick it will make it
show.) Click **Pencil** (though the **Pencil** Button 🖉 is
probably already pressed down by default.) Move the
arrow to the blank page and you'll find you can click and
drag the pencil about to make a drawing. (If nothing
happens, try a right-click.) Try and draw a palm tree. If
you get into a muddle and want to start again, click the
Image Menu and click **Clear** Image. If you can't manage a
palm tree, just make any old squiggle. (To avoid compli-
cations, please postpone having fun with this program

until after this exercise. To find Paint again, all you need is ▐Start – Programs ▸ Accessories ▸ Paint.)

Note that your drawing, just pencilled lines, can also be known as a File or document, and that it consists of data. It must now be named and saved, so click File – Save As. This time we'll **save it into the Holidays Folder**. To do this, click the scroll Button ▼ in the Save in box and choose C. Then click the Holidays Folder which appears below. Click Open, and the Holidays Folder appears in the Save in box, opened in readiness to receive the drawing you are about to name. In the File name box, type in the name Coconut. Click Save. The drawing is now named Coconut, and is saved in the Holidays Folder in the cabinet called C. It reappears, now entitled Coconut-Paint, safe! ✖ it away to return to the C window. Click open the Holidays Folder and there a drawing called Coconut is listed along with Bermuda and Austria. Close the Holidays Folder.

Lists and Details

With the C window open in My Computer, the View Menu offers you, among other things, either **List or Details**. List just gives a list of the Files and Folders contained in the cupboard called C, most of which are of no interest. Details gives you details about them. Also on that Menu is **Arrange Icons ▸**. If you choose by Name, you will see that Arrange Icons by Name is amazing computerspeak for List in numerical order first Folders with names beginning with a number and follow this with a list, in alphabetical order, of those whose names begin with a letter; then do the same with Files. If, with the Details Button clicked, you choose Arrange Icons by Size, you'll see that even a simple picture File is much bigger than a plain text File. (You need a maximised window to have room for all the details.)

Making New Folders
We made a new Folder, Holidays, in the ▭ [C:] window. You can put a new Folder on the Desktop or in any window which can provide storage for it. Right-click over this potential storage place and you will be offered a Menu containing the item New. Click that and then click Folder. ▭ New Folder appears.

Give it a name and remember where you put it. You can open a new Folder in a Folder window like Holidays, because a Folder is a storage place which can itself contain a new Folder – a sub-Folder if you like to call it that. But, if you right-click in a window like WordPad or Solitaire, you'll get different instructions or no instructions, because, though you can put a File into a Folder, you can't put a Folder into a File or a program.

When you are saving a File into a folder, the Save Button on the Save as window may say Open, not Save. That means that a Folder is showing in the window as a possible storage space. Clicking that Open Button opens the Folder ready for accepting the File you are saving.

Go back to the Desktop ready for Exercise 8.

Exercise 8

DRIVES C AND A

The correct computerspeak name for **C**, the cupboard in which we stored our holiday documents, is **Hard disk drive C**. For us beginners, however, it helps to think of it as a *place* where you can store information. Ignore the differences between **C**, [C], [C:] and C:\ which you may see on various windows: they all refer to the same place.

With a double-click, open **C** in the **My Computer** window and there you will see the **Holidays** Folder you put there. Open that Folder with a double-click and there are your three Files, listed in the order you selected from **Arrange Icons** in the **View Menu**.

The computerspeak name for **A** (also known as **drive A**, [A], A:, or A:\) is **3½ Floppy [A:]**. Its main purpose is to copy Files and Folders on to **Floppy disks**. It can also let you see the contents of floppy disks made by other people.

You can make as many copies of a floppy disk as you wish, then you can send them cheaply by post or store them in the bank or in a fireproof safe. Once your stuff is saved onto floppies, you aren't completely ruined if your computer is struck by lightning or stolen by burglars. But, like everything in this ever-changing world, they don't last forever. They hate dust, coffee, gin-and-tonic and even water; but, above all, they hate magnets. Cordless phones and loudspeakers contain magnets, so keep floppy disks away from them. (Loudspeakers supplied by computer dealers are shielded so as not to damage floppies.) Write a name on every floppy you use as one floppy may otherwise be indistinguishable from another.

They come in various sizes. One is 720kB, which stands for 720 kilobytes (a **kilobyte** being 1024 bytes). These are becoming out of date because they are too small. A **byte** is the unit of measurement a computer uses to construct things like words. A commoner size is 1.44MB (MB stands for megabyte, 1024 kilobytes).

Files that show pictures are very greedy for bytes, but words are not. Just look at the Details (clickable on the View Menu of the Holidays window) of your Coconut File. My one took up 218kB compared with 5kB used by Bermuda and Austria. It is because films and music are such gigantic swallowers of bytes that they need special discs (CDs and DVDs) in order to be played on PCs.

Inserting a Floppy Disk
A floppy disk won't fit anywhere else in your machine other than in the floppy disk slot, and if it's the wrong way up it won't go in. Always hold a floppy by its labelled end. If it hasn't got a label, insert the disk with the metallic end first. The disk should be inserted with the round metallic shape facing downwards. To see what's contained in a floppy disk sitting in its slot, double-click My Computer on the Desktop and then double-click 3½ Floppy [A:] in the My Computer window. If there are any Files or

Folders in that A cupboard, they will be listed there.

A floppy disk must be **formatted** before use. Formatting is an initiation ceremony to prepare a floppy for being used in a computer. You can buy IBM formatted disks or you can format them yourself. To format a disk, put a 720kB or 1.44MB unformatted floppy disk into the floppy disk slot. Double-click My Computer on the Desktop. Then single-click the 3½ Floppy Disk icon, (single-click because you don't want to open it, just to use its File Menu.) (If there isn't at this moment a floppy waiting in the slot, your machine may object by grunting with annoyance and displaying a white cross on an angry red background.) Click File, then Format. Choose between 720kB and 1.44MB and click the Full option. Click the Start Button in the window (not the ![Start] Button on the taskbar). Click Close Buttons when they appear. If the disk you put into the slot was a previously formatted disk with data on it, that data will be wiped out during this reformatting, so don't pick up the wrong one by mistake.

Before taking a floppy out of its slot, close the 3½ Floppy [A:] window. Give your machine a moment or two to realise it's gone before putting in another one.

Ordinary floppies with 1.44 megabytes are not capacious enough to contain more than a few pages of material like this book, which has many pictures, each requiring thousands of bytes. Fortunately there are disks available (such as **zip disks**) with capacities like 100 megabytes, but to use them your machine has to be fitted with a special slot and drive. I bless the day I had one installed.

Exercise 9

MOVING AND COPYING
FILES OR FOLDERS

Moving by Cut, Copy and Paste
Just as you can manipulate whatever it is that you have
highlighted – a character, a word or a chunk of text – by
using Cut, Copy or Paste from the Edit Menu, (or by
clicking ✂, 📄 or 📋 on the Toolbar), you can do the
same with a File or Folder in the My Computer window.
You can cut, copy or paste the whole contents of a File by
highlighting all of it with Select All from the Edit Menu,
but you can also cut or copy and paste a File or Folder by
highlighting just its *name*. You can also move a File or
Folder from place to place or copy it elsewhere by dragging it.

Moving by Dragging
We dragged a bit of highlighted text to the Desktop to
make a readily available letterhead. As long as you can
display a bit of window and a bit of Desktop on the same

screen, you can **drag** from one to the other; not just bits of text, but the *contents* of Files or Folders. If you display two windows, or just enough of them, on the same screen, you can drag text, Files or Folders from one to the other. You can also drag an item to a temporary resting place in a corner of the Desktop, open a shrunken window for its destination, and then drag it there from the Desktop.

Dragging to a Floppy Disk
By copying stuff onto a floppy disk you can give it wings to fly away from your desk-bound machine. You can then send it to someone by post. One of the principal reasons, though, for copying onto a floppy is to make a back-up copy of something as insurance against damage to the original. As an example of dragging to a floppy, open the Holidays Folder in C to show the name Austria, and, by manipulating the window – shrinking it with 🗗 or using the double-headed arrow ↕ or ⇖ in its titlebar to drag it out of the way – get 3½ Floppy [A] showing in the My Computer window as well. Provided there is a floppy in the slot waiting to receive it, drag Austria towards 3½ Floppy [A]. As you get near, 3½ Floppy [A] becomes highlighted. (That's how you know you are on target.) Release your clicker and you'll see Austria flying from C to A!

Moving Files to a Floppy Disk by **Send To** ▸
This is by far the slickest way of making a backup copy of a File or Folder on a floppy. First, put a formatted floppy disk into the floppy disk slot to receive what you propose to Send To it. Then, open a window to expose the name of the item you want to make a backup of, say the C window which contains your Holidays Folder. Highlight

Holidays with a single-click – a double-click would open
it, which you don't want to do. Open the File Menu,
choose Send To ▸ and click 3½ Floppy [A]. You can now
watch the contents of the Folder Holidays flying over to
the floppy disk. To see it there you'll have to get back to
3½ Floppy [A:] on the My Computer window and double-
click it open. You'll see there the Austria File you dragged
there and the Holidays Folder you have just performed
Send To ▸ on. Don't forget to label the floppy so that in
future you'll know what it contains. When going from C
to A this way, you don't just move something, you make a
copy of it in A and leave the original behind in C. If,
however, you **press shift when you click Send To ▸**, you
don't leave a copy behind in C but just move it across to
A.

Copying
The rule is that if you move something from one part of C
to another part of C, or from one part of A to another part
of A, you are just moving it; but, if you move something
from **C to A by dragging** or by using Send To ▸, you don't
just move it, you make a copy of it in A and leave the
original behind in C. We saw that you can break this rule
for Send To ▸ by holding down shift. You can also break
it if, when dragging, you use the *right* mouse clicker and
not the *left* one. If you use the right clicker for dragging,
when you release it you're given, among the choices,
Move Here, or **Copy Here**. Click your pick with the left
mouse Button. Decide carefully. It's unwise to leave
unnecessary copies strewn about, because the time will
come when, after an alteration to a copy or its original,
you won't know which is which. It's therefore worth
cultivating the habit of always using the right clicker for

moving Files and Folders and making a careful choice between **Move Here** and **Copy Here**. Don't forget, either, that if you alter an original document in **C** after it's been copied to **A**, the copy in **A** remains unaltered unless recopied. But it's only a second's work to click the document's name, click the **File Menu**, **Send To ▸ 3½ Floppy [A]** and click **Yes** to the question **Would you like to replace the existing File with this one?**

Copying a Whole Floppy Disk
To do this you need to have a formatted disk ready to be copied onto. Put the disk you want to have copied into the floppy disk slot. On the Desktop, double-click **My Computer** and then single-click **3½ Floppy [A]**. On the **File Menu** click **Copy Disk**. You'll see on the Copy Disk window on which appears both **Copy to 3½ Floppy [A]** and **Copy from 3½ Floppy [A]**. Click **Start**. Wait patiently and follow the instructions, not forgetting to label the finished product.

Moving a File or Folder from One Floppy to Another
Cut, **Copy** and **Paste** is at your disposal. You could also drag a File or Folder to the Desktop. Put a different floppy in the slot and drag across the Desktop directly on to **3½ Floppy [A:]** or onto one of its opened windows.

Disk Space Available
When you have more than a few small Files to copy onto a floppy, an attempt at copying may be interrupted by the message **The destination disk is full**. To see what space is available on a floppy disk, go **My Computer – 3½ Floppy [A]** (a single-click) – **File – Properties**. That shows you a

pie chart with the answer. It's surprising how much space
Paint Files occupy. (To see what space is available in C, go
My Computer – C (single-click) – File – Properties.)

To Recap . . .
COMPUTERS ARE KNOWN TO CRASH – KEEP
BACKUP COPIES OF IMPORTANT STUFF ON
FLOPPIES.

To make a back up, use Send To ▶ on the File Menu.
Choose 3½ Floppy [A] and click Yes to the question
Would you like to replace the existing File with this one?
Do the same to a copy already on a floppy to update it.

Exercise 10

FINDING, DELETING AND RESTORING FILES AND FOLDERS

To Find a File or Folder

So far you've made only three Files, so it's easy to find any of them again, but say you had hundreds? No problem. If you remember where you saved a File you know where to look for it. You saved the File **Coconut** in the **Holidays Folder**, stored in the filing cabinet **C**. You could therefore find it by going **My Computer** – 🖥 **[C:]** – 📁 **Holidays** and opening that. The **path** started from **C** and ended with the name of the File. This is the logical route, but not always the most practical, because many shortcuts are available.

One is the **Find** system from the 🔲**Start** Menu. (Do not confuse this with **Find** on the **Edit** Menu, which you used to find the word **bath**.) To find a File, go 🔲**Start**, up to **Find ▶**, across to **Files or Folders** and click. You

now have a window called **Find: All Files**. In the box
called Named, containing the blinking Cursor, type
Coconut, or cOconUt but not Cocoanut. Case sensitivity
doesn't matter, spelling does. Then click the ▾ Button
in the Look in box to decide whether to look in C or A.
(If there's a box called Include subfolders, tick it.)
Decide for the moment to look in C. Click Find Now
and your Coconut File appears. You'd be told that it is
stored in C:\Holidays, and is 218 kilobytes (or something
like that) in size. If you had chosen not C but A,
provided the floppy was in its slot you'd see two Files
called Coconut showing up, the one you dragged to A
and the other contained in the Holidays Folder you Sent
to ▸ A. If you had chosen My Computer in the Look in
box, you'd find all three Coconut Files showing there,
the one in C and the two in A. When maximised, the
Find: All Files window will have room to give you the
date and even the time when the various Coconut Files
were last saved. You can open a File found in the Find:
All Files window by double-clicking on its name.

   You can also find a program in the Find: All Files
window. Try and find Paint that way. But what if you
don't remember the name you gave to a File, say to that
palm tree drawing, and have even forgotten that you
have a Folder called Holidays? There are several
solutions.

1.   Open a window, say C, showing the names of Files
     which might include the palm tree drawing. Then
     open the View Menu and select **Arrange Icons** ▸ By
     Name. This puts the items in alphabetical order and
     might remind you of its name. Among the dozens
     listed there Coconut shows up.

2. If that doesn't help, try **Arrange Icons ▶ By Type**. This would immediately show up any picture File because all are grouped together.

3. **Arrange Icons ▶ By Size** might be helpful, and so might **By Date**, if you had an idea when you last had the drawing of the palm tree on view.

4. If you click **Browse** on the Find: All Files window, you will be shown all sorts of possible locations and you can select a likely one in which to look.

5. At the top of that window is a tab called **Date**, or **Date modified**, which can narrow down a search by specifying the date a File was last changed.

6. Using the **Name & Location** tab you can also type something memorable in the box **Containing text**.

Once a File or Folder's name appears in the Find: All Files window, you can double-click it open, or drag it elsewhere. Other ways of finding a File are mentioned in Exercise 11, page 77.

Renaming a File or Folder.
To rename a File or Folder you must find its name in a window (the Find: All Files window will do). If you wanted to change the name **Bermuda** in the **Holidays Folder** window, you first have to click **Bermuda** to high-light it and then give the name a second click (or press the **F2 key**) to make the name blink. (If the second click followed too soon after the first one, the machine would interpret this as a double-click and open the File, but that's not what you want.) In the blinking name box, type a new name, say **Barbados**, followed by an **extension** that describes its type, in this case **.doc**. That is the extension which shows that it had its origin in WordPad. The three

letters of an extension must be preceded immediately by a full stop. If you changed **Bermuda.doc** to **Barbados. doc**, you'd be in trouble because you'd put a space between the full stop and the **doc**. Confirm your new name by pressing **Enter** on the keyboard or by clicking elsewhere.

A name can be as long as 255 characters. If you try and use any of the characters \ / : * ? " < >, your machine will tell you these won't work. If, when trying to rename a File, you are presented with an exclamation mark and the phrase **access is denied**, this usually means that the File is already opened. If open, it will have its Button on the taskbar, so right-click the Button and click **Close**.

Deleting a File or Folder
To do this you must first find its name and highlight it. As happened with renaming a File, access will be denied if the File is currently open. If so, close it. When the name is highlighted, click **Delete** on the **File Menu**, or the delete icon on the Toolbar, or press the **Delete** key on the keyboard. The **Delete** key works anywhere, deleting any-thing that's highlighted: an icon on the Desktop, a File listed in a window or a piece of highlighted text.

Deletion transfers a File to a transit camp called the **Recycle Bin**. (It **deletes permanently** only if you press **Delete** + **Shift**.) To see the Recycle Bin working, open your **Holidays** Folder via **My Computer** – **C** – **Holidays**, then highlight and Delete all three Files there, one by one. As you delete, you'll be asked to confirm this intention. Shut any windows hiding the Recycle Bin on your Desk-top (or reveal the Desktop by clicking the 🖮 Button on your taskbar, if you have one there) and double-click **Recycle Bin** to open it. Your three Files are there.

If the same File exists in different places – a copy in **A**, for instance, and the original in C – deleting it in one place won't delete it in another. Your machine only does what it's told; it can't read your thoughts.

If the Recycle Bin icon is visible on the Desktop, you can drag things onto it there rather than highlighting and deleting them. To find a File in a crowded Recycle Bin don't forget its View Menu, which offers **Arrange Icons**.

Unlike documents in C, which, when deleted, go to the Recycle Bin, an **item deleted from A** doesn't have that safeguard and disappears at one go. Beware! Even an immediate Undo last command won't rescue it.

Restoring a Deleted File
Highlight the File to be restored in the Recycle Bin window and click Restore on the File Menu. You can also drag a File out of the Bin into a window or onto the Desktop.

Permanent Removal from the Recycle Bin
To get rid of a File or Folder from the Recycle Bin, highlight it and press the Delete key. To empty the Recycle Bin at one go, open its File Menu and click **Empty Recycle Bin**. Prune your Recycle Bin of rubbish whenever you have the courage. It occupies valuable space.

If you delete a Folder, it may sometimes appear in the Recycle Bin not as a Folder but as a list of all the Files it contains. To restore each one separately may be tedious but you can deal in **groups of Files**. This is looking forward to the day when you have lots of them. To handle more than one File at a time, click one to highlight it. With the Shift key pressed, click another File, separated from the first one by others. This will highlight not just the two

Files you've clicked but all the Files between as well. To make an assorted bunch of Files you want to handle into a group, hold down the Ctrl key each time you highlight a File and they will all remain highlighted and can be dealt with as a bunch.

You can handle, in either of these two ways, groups of Files for deleting, copying or moving in other areas too. You can use the **Select All** Menu item in Edit to select all the Files in one Folder.

Exercise 11

SHORTCUTS

You could find the File Coconut by looking for it where you saved it, which was in the Holidays Folder you made in the C window. You could therefore reach it by going Desktop – My Computer – ▭ [C:] and clicking ▨ Holidays. But because you have recently worked on it, a quicker way is available. This is to go ⊞Start and up to **Documents** ▸, because this automatically lists the fifteen Files you have most recently worked on. Look at Documents ▸ and there will be the names of the three Files you have made so far. You can single-click one to open it, just as you can single-click to select any item on any Menu.

To empty Documents, go ⊞Start – Settings ▸ Taskbar – Start Menu Programs (a tab at the top of the taskbar Properties window) and click Clear – OK. To get a File listed in Documents, just opening it is enough, because a moment of attention is all that's required to qualify an item for inclusion as a recently worked document.

Making a Shortcut from the Desktop to a File or Folder
You could left-click and drag the name of a File or Folder
from any window onto a bit of Desktop, from where it
could be opened by double-clicking. At first sight, this is a
useful shortcut. But that File or Folder would be moved
outright onto the Desktop, leaving nothing behind. From
the Desktop it might even get sent by accident to the
Recycle Bin, only to be permanently deleted when the
Recycle Bin was next emptied. But if you used the right-
clicker for dragging, you could choose **Copy Here**, so that
the original would stay where it was and only a duplicate
version planted on the Desktop. Dragging with the right
clicker offers:

Move Here
Copy Here
Create Shortcut(s) Here

Copy Here with NFS File Translation...

Cancel

You might feel that copying was playing safe, by making
an extra backup but, as you have been warned, scattering
copies about can lead to confusion. Keep backups on
special floppy disks kept for that purpose.

It is better to make the other choice given to you when
you right-click for dragging, **Create Shortcut Here**. Try
this, by dragging the name of the File Coconut onto

your Desktop with your right clicker and choosing
Create Shortcut Here. This leaves the original safely
where it was and puts just an icon on the Desktop,
which you will see is labelled **Shortcut to Coconut** and
maybe has a little shortcut arrow symbol in its corner.
Double-clicking it opens the drawing, but deleting it
deletes only the shortcut, not the drawing itself.

Shortcut from Desktop to Your 3½ Floppy [A:]
Creating too many shortcuts on your Desktop may clutter
it, but this one you may find useful. Go Desktop – **My
Computer** and, with the right clicker, drag **3½ Floppy [A:]**
onto the Desktop. Click **Create Shortcut Here**. A double-
click on it there will open it.

Shortcut from One Folder to Another Folder or File
You can park a shortcut to a File or Folder temporarily
on Desktop and drag it from the Desktop onto any
window. You can then go direct from that window to the
item you've made a shortcut to. Or you can create a
shortcut to an item in any window by dragging that item's
name onto the window with a right-click drag and choosing **Create Shortcut Here**. This technique would be useful
if you had a Folder containing many other Folders, each
containing various chapters of a book, one of which you
constantly referred to. You could drag the chapter on
which you were working onto its mother Folder and
create a shortcut to it there.

Shortcut from the Start Menu to a Program
Items on the **Start** Menu are shortcuts already. The
'longcut', for instance, to Solitaire, is Desktop – **My Computer** – 📁 [C:] – 📁 Windows – 📁 Start Menu –

▦ Programs – ▦ Accessories – ▦ Games – Solitaire.
(There's even a shortcut from ▦Start to ▦ Programs in
the Start Menu window. It goes: right-click on ▦Start –
Open.) Being the real things and not just shortcuts, you
can drag these programs about (which you can't do with
just their names on the ▦Start Menu.) You could drag the
program Solitaire or the program Calculator onto your
Desktop to make a shortcut from there. You could also
drag and drop a program like Calculator onto the ▦Start
Button. Then, when you clicked ▦Start, **Calculator** would
show in the first part of the Menu and not on the far right.
(To **remove an item** such as Calculator from the Start
Menu, go ▦Start – Settings ▸ Taskbar – Start Menu
Programs (a tab at the top of the Taskbar Properties
window) – Remove. Click Calculator in the list you are
offered and then Remove again. It's gone.)

Shortcut on Switching On
The ultimate shortcut is to have something automatically
showing on the screen when you switch on. For this, go
My Computer – ▭ [C:] – ▦ Windows – ▦ Start
Menu – ▦ Programs. Click ▦ Programs and look for
the Folder called ▦ StartUp and double-click that. If
you drag a program or a File into the **StartUp window**,
it will be ready-opened when you next switch on. Like
everything currently active, it will be represented by
Buttons on the taskbar, so you can switch from one to
the other.

   To get rid of one of these shortcuts, delete its name in
the StartUp window. (Don't confuse the ▦ Start Menu
(in the ▦ Windows which contains the programs you see
when you click the ▦Start Button on the taskbar) with the
▦ StartUp in the ▦ Programs.)

Desktop Icons Misbehaving?

Right-clicking on your Desktop will give you a Menu for controlling the positions of the icons there. If, for instance, when you try to drag icons about the Desktop, they won't budge, you may be under the influence of Auto Arrange. Right-click on the Desktop and click **Arrange Icons ▸ Auto Arrange** so as to remove the tick mark ✔ alongside it and the icons will then obey your will. You can tidy up icons there, and make more desk space available, by making a new Folder on the Desktop and dragging them inside. (To remind you: right-click on the Desktop and select **New – Folder**. Type in a name and press **Enter** to confirm.)

Exercise 12

WINDOWS EXPLORER

In the last exercise we opened Folder after Folder, each containing other Folders. Starting from Desktop, we went My Computer – 🖛 [C:] – 📁 Windows – 📁 Start Menu – 📁 Programs – 📁 Accessories – 📁 Games. Do this again, starting from Desktop and finishing up with 📁 Games. By pressing the backspace key ◄—, you can now retrace your steps. In this way you can go backwards from 📁 Games to My Computer, passing on the way 📁 Accessories, 📁 Programs, 📁 Start Menu, 📁 Windows and 🖛 [C:]. If you try to backspace again to Desktop, you'll be told that you're at the top level. My Computer was the starting point for getting from the top of the mountainous pile of stuff in your computer down to Solitaire at the bottom.

You don't have to start from My Computer to view the whole shebang. There's another starting point for seeing what's in the valley below. This is Windows Explorer. This you find on the Programs Menu offered by the 🏁 Start Button. Click open Windows Explorer and you are given a comprehensive view of the whole contents of your computer.

This window has two **panes**, one on the left and one on the right. (You can drag the dividing line between them to right or left with the double-headed arrow ◄—► which appears if you put your ▷ on the dividing line.) Make sure the left pane is scrolled to its top, either by dragging its slider upwards or clicking on the ▲ Button at the top of the scroll bar. Click an item in the left pane – [C:] or the Recycle Bin, or a Folder such as Windows – and its contents will show up in the right pane. When clicked, a Folder icon ▢ in the left pane will be seen to open, now ▢, its contents now showing up in the right pane. To close the Folder, click something else in the left pane – the right pane can display only one choice at a time.

In the left hand pane you will see **plus signs** +. These are signs which say "There's a lot more inside". Click the + adjoining an item and it will show its subdivisions and change to –. (Click the **minus sign** – to reverse this process.)

Lists and Details
Since the right hand pane of the Explorer window gives you lists of Files and Folders, you can open the View Menu and click either the **List** or the **Details** option. Also on that Menu is **Arrange Icons**. You will remember that if you choose By Name you will see that Arrange Icons By Name is computerspeak for First list in numerical order Folders with names beginning with a number and follow this with a list, in alphabetical order, of those whose names begin with a letter; then do the same with Files. This numerical and alphabetical arrangement can make it easy to find what you want. Having gone down

the mountain from left to right on Explorer you can go
back up, Folder by Folder, by using the **backspace key**
◄—.

Sorting Files and Folders
In the Explorer window, as with other windows and on
the Desktop, you can drag Files in and out of Folders, and
you can drag one Folder into another. If you reduce the
size of the window so as to reveal some Desktop, you can
drag a File onto the Desktop and move it again later into
any old window. You can drag from **A** to **C** or from **C** to
A, but this change to or from a floppy disk is a copying
action unless you hold Shift down as you drag.

If you find that you constantly begin work with it,
**Windows Explorer can be safely left open when shutting
down**. It will be open when you next switch on.

Don't be daunted by the apparent complexity of
Windows Explorer compared with the My Computer
approach. The Explorer window only looks complicated
because there's so much in it. Much of the complexity of
the My Computer method or the Windows Explorer
method of listing Files and Folders can be avoided by
saving Files directly onto the Desktop.

Until you have vast amounts of Files and Folders to
cope with, when you have a new File and want to save it
somewhere, you can click, when the Save As window
comes up, Desktop in the Save in box. Give the new File
a name in the File Name box, click Save, and it will then
appear on your Desktop, instantly available just by
double-clicking it there. If there are lots of such Files,
personal letters for instance, make a right click on your
Desktop and make a new Folder, name it Personal Letters and drag the letters already on Desktop into it. A new

letter can also go straight into that same Folder when you first save it. To do this, click Desktop in the **Save As** window, double-click the Folder listed there called **Personal Letters**, type a name for the letter in the **File Name** box, click **Save** and the letter will be stored as an item in the Personal Letters Folder on your Desktop.

Exercise 13

HELP

A *general* **Help** program is found on the **⊞Start** Menu. **Help** *specific* to a particular program is found as a Menu in the Menu bar of the window of that program. **Help** in the Solitaire window helps Solitaire; **Help** on the Paint window helps Paint. **Help** Menus offer tabs such as **Contents**, **Index**, and **Find** or **Search**.

The **Contents** *Tab*
There's useful stuff hidden in this section, but there are easier ways of looking at it.

The **Index** *Tab*
Index in the *general* **Help** program produces a vast list of subjects, most of which will never concern you. To get help, type in the box where the Cursor is blinking the first few letters of a title recognised by the machine. Type **bin** and you get nowhere, because those three letters are not the first letters of a recognised title, but type **recycle**, or even just **recyc**, and **Recycle Bin** will be highlighted. Click

Display and more choices will be offered. Choose **Empty-ing the Recycle Bin** and then click **Display** to see how to do this – as if you didn't know already!

The **Find** *Tab in Windows 95*
This is the third version of the word **Find** we have come across. First there was **Find ▶** in the **Start** Menu, for finding Files or Folders, and second there was **Find** in the **Edit** Menu of WordPad, where you were invited to type a word you wanted to search for. We found the word **Bath** this way. This **Help** version of **Find** searches for a word that appears in the title of a **Help** subject. The first time you use it, the **Find Setup Wizard** will appear. Click **Next** and follow the instructions.

The **Search** *Tab in Windows 98*
Search looks for a word that figures in the title of a subject. Type the word **recycle**, click **List topics** and, because **recycle** is part of a known title, you're given choices – one of which is **To empty the Recycle Bin**. Highlight and click **Display**. To look for something else, type in the new word.

Right-Clicking for Help
Sometimes a right-click over something produces a **What's this?** question, which, when clicked, gives an answer. Try this on the Calculator window. (**Start** – **Programs** – **Accessories** – **Calculator**.)

Exercise 14

CLOCK AND DATE

If the digital **clock** is not showing on your taskbar, go **Start** – Settings ▸ Taskbar and tick ✔ Show Clock.

Today's date can be seen if you rest your mouse arrow on the clock showing on the right of the taskbar and wait.

To adjust the time or the date, open the Date/Time Properties window by double-clicking the clock on the taskbar. Click the Date & Time tab, if it's not already showing, and make the necessary changes in the white boxes.

Your computer has been programmed automatically to take care of the changeover between **Summer and Winter time**. You can satisfy yourself that this is so by opening the Date/Time Properties window and clicking the Time Zone tab. You'll see that Automatically adjust clock for daylight saving changes is ticked and you'll be agreeably surprised to see, in Spring and Autumn, a message on your screen confirming that this has been done.

Exercise 15

CHARMAP

Charmap is short for character map. It provides characters which aren't available on the keyboard. If you intend to type in **French or other languages**, invest in an appropriate keyboard or software, because it can be tedious to rely on the Charmap for typing words like tête à tête or señorita. But Charmap is good for the occasional use. Find it by going 🪟Start – Programs ▸ Accessories ▸ (and maybe System Tools ▸).

Once in a document, open the Character Map window and point your mouse ⤵ on the character you want and click. Then click Select and then Copy. The character – or characters – is now stored on your invisible clipboard, waiting to be pasted when you switch back to the document on which you're working. Choose an insertion point and click Paste.

Note the name in the Font box in the Charmap window. Different fonts give you a different set of characters. Have a look at what they offer you. If, when you paste, the **Charmap character differs from what you expected**, the font you copied it from is not the same as the one you are pasting into. Once you have pasted in the new character, highlight it and change the font from the font box on the Toolbar.

Note also the **Keystroke** box in the bottom right hand corner of a Charmap. The keystroke, for instance, for the è in très bien is **Alt + 0232**. To use it, keep **Alt** pressed while you press the number on the keys on the right of your keyboard. When you release Alt, the **keystroke character from Charmap** appears. As the ½ of 3½ **Floppy** recurs in this book, I have jotted down the keystroke **Alt + 0189**. For this technique to work, the **Num Lock** key must be pressed so that its light is lit up on the keyboard.

Some other useful **accents** are: **Alt**+129=ü, +130=é, +131=â, +133=à, +134=å +135=ç +136=ê, +138=è, +139=ï, +145=æ, +147=ô and +184=©.

Exercise 16

PAINT

The program Paint is found by going 🎨Start – **Programs** ▶ **Accessories** ▶ **Paint**. An art gallery would be needed to illustrate all that the Paint program can do.

When you open Paint, the **Tool Box** is probably showing. If it isn't, a ✔ is required in the **View** Menu. The same goes for the **Color Box**. If you put the tip of your mouse arrow exactly at the very edge of the tool box or the color box, you can drag them about. The pencil Button ✏ is already, that is to say, by default, pressed in for action. You draw by dragging the mouse.

Rest your mouse arrow on each of the Buttons along the tool box in turn, allowing each one enough time to display its function. You can make the drawing easier to see on the screen by magnifying a section of it by putting the magnifier 🔍 over it. To reverse the magnification, click **View** – **Zoom** – **Normal Size**.

When you have produced something you like, save it before doing any more experimenting which might spoil it.

Until there is something selected on your drawing

board, **Cut** and **Copy** on the **Edit** Menu will be dimmed
out. Selecting something in Paint is what is often called
highlighting in Files containing text. To select a drawing,
click the **Select** Button on the tool box. Dragging the
mouse pointer ╀, now cross-shaped, from top left of the
drawing to bottom right will draw a rectangle to enclose
it. What is in the rectangle is now selected. To select only
part of a drawing, click **Free-Form Select**. Once an area is
selected, you can copy and paste it elsewhere or drag it
about the drawing board. To delete what you've selected,
put the pointer in the dotted rectangle and press **Delete**.
To get rid of such selections, click anywhere.

The ⬚**A** Button, when pointed at, declares itself to be
Text. If you click it, your mouse pointer ╀, when dragged
from upper left to lower right will make an oblong in
which typed letters will be accepted. You need the text
Toolbar for this. If it's not showing, click the **View** Menu
and give **Text Toolbar** a tick. You will be offered a choice
of font, point size, underline, italic and bold. There are
two squares to the left of the color box. To print in a
colour, left-click the colour on the Color Box and the
front square will show that colour. If you right-click a
colour, the back square, usually white, will change to that
colour. The background of the text rectangle will now
change to that colour. To get rid of a text rectangle, but
leave what you've typed, click anywhere.

If you want to use the **Undo** command but the **Edit**
Menu which contains it is hidden by the text Toolbar,
instead of clicking away the text Toolbar, it is easier to
revert to the pre-mouse era and type **Ctrl+Z** which is the
keyboard shortcut for **Undo**.

If you want to set the size of the picture when printed,
choose **Attributes** in the **Image** Menu and fill in the

required dimensions. You can alter the size of a drawing by selecting it and using the Image Menu.

To colour a space enclosed within a line, for example a circle drawn with the Ellipse tool, click on a colour and on the Fill with colour Button. Move over the space and click there. If more space than you expect gets coloured, there's probably a gap in the line around the space, allowing the paint to leak out. If you can't see a gap, click on the magnifier and click again to find the leak.

Trouble-Shooting in Paint
If your screen remains blank with only the mouse arrow ↖ showing on it, do basic first aid. Click the left clicker and, if that doesn't work, the right.

If nothing appears when you draw, perhaps what you are drawing is in the same colour as the background. You can do this deliberately, for instance, by clicking white as a colour and using the Brush to erase other colours on a white background.

Exercise 17

PRINTING

Ask whoever installs your PC to install a printer at the same time. It can be a daunting procedure because you have to plug it in to the back of your machine and may have to follow 'jargonese' instructions.

Print Preview (Not always available)
This item on the File Menu of a WordPad document (or a Button 🔍 on the Toolbar) will show what the printed page will look like.

Page Setup
This item on the File Menu of a WordPad document will offer a choice of paper size, a choice of margin width, and whether you want portrait ☐ or landscape ☐ orientation. (On other word-processing systems, look in the File Menu for items like Document properties.)

wysiwyg
This means "What You See Is What You Get". What

your printer prints may vary in size from what's on your screen. A change of point size can counteract this so as to achieve "wysiwyg".

To Start Printing
If you choose the print Button *from the Toolbar*, printing may start at once. If, however, you choose Print *from the* File *Menu*, the Print window gives you a choice for selecting the particular pages of a document that you want printed, the number of copies and the quality of print. Different printers will offer different options for printing, so it is best to refer to the handbook which accompanied your printer.

Exercise 18

CDs AND CD-ROMs

To play a CD (**Compact Disc**) you need a CD-ROM slot to put it in (usually known as **Drive [D:]**) and loudspeakers. ROM stands for Read Only Memory, a computerspeak way of saying that a CD-ROM can recite from memory but can't learn anything new.

Playing a Music CD
Press the Button just below the CD-ROM slot and a tray will come out or a door will open. (Other controls there refer to an extension loudspeaker.) Put a CD on the tray, labelled side up, and press the Button to make the tray go back into the machine, carrying the disk with it. The CD driver may be sluggish and you may have to wait several seconds until the little light below the slot stops flickering and the music starts.

A CD Player Button appears in the taskbar as the program begins. This is a minimised version of the CD Player window. Click it and the Window itself appears on the screen. Rest your mouse arrow on the Button and it will announce itself as **Play**. Next to it is a Button for **Pause** and next to that a Button for **Stop**.

When the music starts automatically in this way, **auto-play** is operating. If you don't want a CD to start playing automatically, don't put it in the slot until you're ready for it. (To disable autoplay more permanently, follow the rather tedious route prescribed by Help in the CD Player window.)

If the music doesn't start automatically, check that **Mute** isn't ticked. To see Mute, click the little triangular yellow icon near to the digital clock on your taskbar called Volume. If Mute is ticked ✔, untick it with a click. (Ticking Mute comes in useful to silence a CD when the phone rings or to stop aural inanities coming from a CD-ROM.) You can drag the slider to adjust volume.

If you ✖ the CD Player window or close it by other means, the program shuts down, but, if you just minimise it down to the taskbar, the music keeps going.

If you are driven mad by the wrong track being played, click Options in the CD Player window to see if Random is ticked.

Playing a CD-ROM

Whereas music CDs play sounds only, CD-ROMs may include sounds, text and illustrations. Some CD-ROMs come with instructions printed on the packaging. Most supply on-screen instructions when you start playing them. These step-by-step instructions are known as a wizard, so all you have to do is to glance at the screen to see what it says and press Next.

When a piece of software from a CD-ROM, such as that in Windows 95, 98 or word-processing programs, is needed at all times, the **software** from these CD-ROMs should be **installed**, that is to say, incorporated into your machine by being transferred on to its **hard drive**.

To install anything, put the CD in and follow the instructions that appear on the screen. (If nothing happens, go to My Computer and double-click on (D:). To remove something from the hard drive, follow the uninstallation program, if there is one. Otherwise go ⊞Start –
Settings ▸ – Control Panel – Add/Remove programs. Scroll to find the program and click Remove.

Even if you install, only temporarily, CD-ROM software, such as a game, and then uninstall it, doing this sometimes still leaves your machine cluttered up with a residue of unwanted Files. They don't do any harm, so only delete them if you know what you're doing.

If there is **no response** from a CD-ROM, press on the Button below the CD slot, wait for the tray to come out and then press the Button again. That will restart it.

Changing the Screen Resolution

Sometimes a piece of software which you install prefers a larger screen than you can offer it, making necessary a change in **screen resolution**. In that case you need the program called Display, which is on the Control Panel window (Start – Settings ▸ Control Panel). Click the Settings tab on the Display window and drag the Desktop area slider from Less to More, probably from 640 by 480 **pixels** (little dots which occupy the whole of your screen like the dots on a newspaper picture.), to a larger number on the right. That means that more pixels, smaller ones, can be crammed onto the same-sized screen. Then click any OK or Yes which appears. Reverse the process when you want to revert to normal, starting from the Settings tab on the Display window.

Looking After Your CDs

Keep CDs protected when not in use by keeping them in their boxes or in plastic envelopes. Grease from fingers can confuse the laser beam which scans them.

Exercise 20

WHAT IS THE INTERNET?

The world-wide network of telephones is such that you can telephone anybody with a telephone anywhere on Planet Earth. A computer connected to a telephone can also communicate with any other computer connected to a telephone, anywhere on Planet Earth. That world-wide network of computers, connected to each other by telephone wires, is the basis of the Internet.

The Internet is not just an empty network, because people use it as a display board on which to stick things. Anybody joined up to the Internet can see what's been stuck there. This part of the Internet is called the World Wide Web, the www. What is on display, like the postcards in the window of the local shop, reflects human supply and demand. The www is a library, an art gallery, a music library, a notice board, a porn shop, a shopping mall, a debating society, a newspaper, a lonely hearts club, a mail-order catalogue, a conference of professors, a sporting stadium, a gaming gallery, a railway time-table, a theatre box office, an estate agent – you name it. It is made up of what people have put onto it.

To do this they have each set up a **web-site** and given it an address so that other people can find it. If you did this to advertise your old sofa-bed, everybody joined to the Internet becomes a potential customer. Setting up a web-site requires specialist skills which are beyond the scope of this book.

You can't telephone anybody direct without going through a telephone exchange, even if it's an automatic one. Your computer, likewise, needs an intermediary. It is called an ISP, an **Internet Service Provider**. So if you want to get connected to the Internet, your first need is an ISP connected to you by telephone. You can use an existing telephone line, but it can't communicate with your ISP at the same time as being used as an ordinary telephone, so the two functions must take turns. Busy people have an additional telephone line installed, dedicated to computer use.

The Modem

The gadget in (or plugged into) your computer which connects you by telephone to your ISP is called a **modem**. On rare occasions it may get damaged if a thunderstorm strikes while it is connected to the outside world by a telephone line, even if your computer is unplugged from the mains. It works by translating the digital electrical signals of your computer into signals which can be sent along a telephone line. When they reach their destination they are translated back to the digital electrical signals understood by computers.

Internet Service Providers

There are dozens of them. There is no way you can be sure

that the ISP you chose is the best one for you because they are all different. Some charge you by the hour, some by the month, some have different rates according to the time of day, some are free and earn their keep by advertising, some are fast, some are slow, some suit occasional users, some suit persistent users and so on. No matter; you can easily change later on to another one. Take advantage of the facilities offered by your ISP, such as parental control to protect your children from the pornography which flourishes World Wide.

If you aren't provided with an ISP's software in your PC package, ask a friend to recommend one. Read carefully any literature that comes with the installation CD-ROM and note its helpline telephone number in case you get stuck. To start again, perform **Uninstall** (see index).

Installing an ISP's Software
Right-click on any Buttons on your taskbar and click **Close** to clear them all away, and, when you have some time to spare, put into the slot the CD-ROM provided by the ISP. (A CD-ROM often starts automatically when it goes into the machine. If it's in the machine, but not working, press the Button below the slot, wait for the tray to come out and then press the Button again to send it back in.) You are going to install this software onto your hard disk. Follow very carefully the instructions on your screen (the '**wizard**'). Make a note of your username and password in case you get stuck and have to start again.

'Signing up' is what you do when you register with an ISP. (Signing on is connecting to the Internet, also known as being on-line, being connected or logged on.) If you get stuck, start again and have another go. If the installation is complete but it still doesn't work, uninstall it and start again, if necessary telephoning the helpline.

Once an ISP's software has been installed, its icon will probably appear on your Desktop or on your taskbar. Double-click it and you will be shown a browser. Here is one, **Internet Explorer**, the one that comes with Windows 95, 98 and 2000:

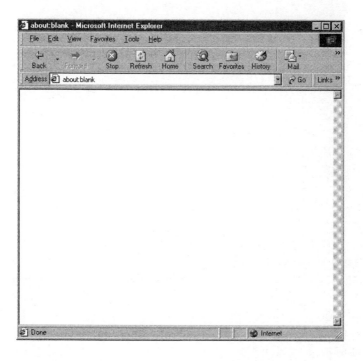

There are others, such as Netscape. A **browser** is a program which allows you to view the Internet. It has a row of icons – a dashboard of switches for choosing what

you want to do with the Internet. Some of them will be
dimmed out unless you are on-line.

Going On-line
Click the ISP icon on your Desktop. You should see
something like this:

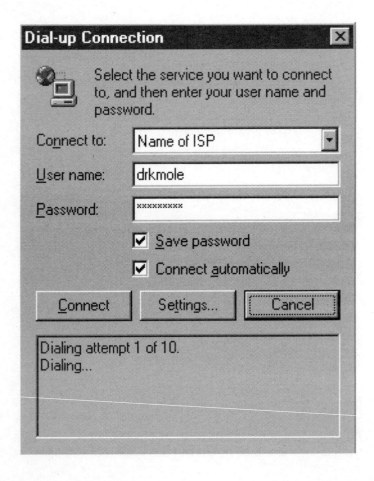

If the **Save Password** box in that Dial-up Connection window is ticked, you won't have to type in your password every time you go on-line. If **Connect automatically** is ticked, you will go on-line when you click your ISP icon on the Desktop, or when you press **Enter** after typing a web-site address. If you're not on-line and wish to be so, you may have to look for **Connect** or **Go On-line** and click there.

To see what's on a **web-site**, type its address, if you know it, in the **Address** or **Location** box on your browser. A web-site may consist of a **page** or many pages. Its address starts with **http://www** although you can just type www and the rest will be added automatically by the browser. The address must be typed exactly; a space, or a comma instead of a full stop, will spoil it.

Press the **Enter** key, and the information at that address gets **downloaded** onto your screen. What appears is the first page at that address. Clicking something underlined or highlighted on a web page – a **link** – will open another page.

The controls on your browser are for manipulating what's now on your screen. Here are some of the controls on Internet Explorer:

Once you have clicked through a few pages on a web-site, you may wish to return to those previously visited. To do this, click the **Back** button ⬅. Once you have clicked **Back**, you may click **Forward** ➡ to return to those pages already visited.

⏹ Click **Stop** if the pages of a web-site are aggravatingly slow in appearing (in being downloaded). You can stop the process with the **Stop Button** and either click 🔄 **Refresh**, or go to a different web-site. (You could ask your dealer to install a faster modem to speed things up.)

[icon] A **Search icon** on a browser will allow you to search the Web for web-sites containing a **keyword** which you have typed in. It may not find what you want, but may be a simple route to start looking for something.

[icon] **Favorites** lets you record a web-site address which you can find quickly next time you go on-line. To do this, have it downloaded, i.e. showing on your screen, click Favorites and then click add to. When you next go on-line and click Favorites, the one you have added to your list will be shown there for you to click open.

[icon] Click Mail when you want to go into e-mail mode. (See page 109.)

[icon] Clicking Print prints what you see on screen.

Search Engines

There are dozens of these, accessible by typing in their www addresses. They scour the web for topics. What they find depends what they have been furnished with, so results vary.

Try typing, in the address box on the browser, the address www.yahoo.co.uk, a search engine. A page will appear containing a query box where you can type a word or subject which you wish to find information about on the Internet. Pressing Enter or clicking Search will open a page containing the results of your search – a list of web-sites which contain the word or words that you entered in the query box. Click on one of these and you will be taken to that web-site. Try typing Elliot Right Way Books in the www.google.com search engine query box. Here you have two options: Google Search or I'm Feeling Lucky. Try searching using both of these. Go down to the bottom of the Google.com page and you will see **Search tips**. Click that and there appears a page of tips on improving your method of searching which could save yourself a lot of trouble. At the bottom of their search results pages, both the Yahoo page and the Google page list the names of other search engines to try.

Storing What You've Downloaded
When a web-site is showing on your screen, click **Save As** on the **File** Menu, or the **Save** icon, and treat what's on your screen as you would a File you wanted to save.

Usenet
This is the name of a collection of Newsgroups. As these may have nothing to do with news, this is the misleading name for what are discussion groups, interested in any subject from pigeon racing to philosophy. They communicate mostly by e-mail. There are at least 25,000 of them.

There are also Chat Rooms (sometimes called channels), web-sites where people can type in conversations. There used to be pen-pals; now there are Internet pals.

To learn more about these things, look at a web-site like www.dejanews.com or use a search engine.

E-mail
E-mail is a method of sending text, images or programs along telephone lines, via the Internet. To engage in e-mail you must use an e-mail program, or mail client. The one supplied with Internet Explorer is called **Outlook Express**. The Netscape browser comes with a mail client called Netscape Messenger.

Sending E-mail
Look for the icon **Mail**, **New Msg** or **New Mail**. Clicking one of these gives you a blank area for you to type in your

message. These icons are clickable before you connect to
the Internet, so that you can compose your message at
leisure without paying for the time taken. You can also
type your message in your word-processing program and,
using Select and Copy, paste it into your e-mail window.

Practise the art of sending e-mails by addressing one
to yourself. You will be given an e-mail address by your
ISP when you sign up with one. In the To box of the
e-mail window, type in the **e-mail address** of the person
you're sending it to. An e-mail address looks like
joebloggs@provider.com. It begins with a name – note
that there are no spaces anywhere in joebloggs – followed
by an @ (pronounced 'at') followed by the name of an
Internet Service Provider. This is followed by a full stop
and other letters such as com or co.uk. Type something in
the Subject box so that in future you can distinguish this
e-mail from others. Either leave the cc box blank or type
in it the e-mail address of someone you want to send a
carbon copy to. To send a **copy to another e-mail address**,
without letting the original recipient know that you are
doing so, type the second address in the bcc (blind carbon
copy) box. Remember the slick **Tab key** ⇄ when jumping
from box to box.

Now that you've composed your message off-line,
click Send and it will be put into your **Outbox**. Click
and then click Connect in the **Dial-up Connection** box
which then appears. When your e-mail has been sent, a
copy will remain in your Sent folder.

When e-mailing a fellow member of an ISP, you may be
able to click Read out-going mail, highlight the name of
the e-mail concerned and click Show status. You will then
be told even at what time your e-mail was read.

If you want to send a picture you have to attach it to

your e-mail as a separate File called an **attachment**. To do this click Attach on your e-mail form. Find the File you wish to attach from the Look in window. Click Attach and send the e-mail in the usual way.

It is helpful to have a separate e-mail icon clickable on your Desktop. See page 77 to remind you how to make a shortcut.

Receiving E-mail
Your new e-mail messages are stored by your Internet Service Provider until you go on-line to check if there are any waiting for you. Once you have checked for new e-mail, it will be listed in your Inbox Folder. You can then go off-line and read it at your leisure.

To reply to an e-mail, highlight its name in the Inbox, then click on the Reply icon. Type your reply and click Send.

If the original e-mail that you received was sent to more than one person, you can click on Reply All, so that everyone who got the original message can receive your reply.

To pass an e-mail you've received on to another person, highlight the message and click on the Forward icon, then type in the recipient's e-mail address in the To box and click Send.

In order to **view an attachment** to an e-mail, you need to download it, to get it into your machine from the outside world. First you must have on screen the e-mail to which it is attached. Then click the paperclip icon in the right-hand corner. You will be asked whether you want to open it or save it. You are now in the same position as you were when, with the Save As window open, you chose a storage site for a new document. Note the name of the attached File and the Folder where you choose to store it. Click **Save**. Then you can find the document by clicking its icon on the Desktop, by **Find Files or Folders** on the **Start** Menu or by following the path to it, Folder by Folder as described on page 71. You can then open it and see it on screen. If the attached File is different in type from your usual ones, there might be problems in viewing it but these are beyond the scope of this guide. Trawl your ISP information material or use its helpline phone number.

When opening e-mail attachments, you must always be aware of the risks posed by viruses. Many viruses are sent by people who do not realise that they are sending them, and often they can do a lot of harm to your computer. One way to arm yourself against this threat is to invest in some anti-virus software which will detect any known viruses contained in an e-mail attachment (or on any disks which you put into the computer) and eradicate them. Another way is always to be very cautious when receiving attachments, especially those with suspicious-sounding file names. If you receive an e-mail with an attachment which you think may contain a virus, delete the e-mail without opening the attachment and contact the person who sent it to you.

Exercise 21

UNSOLICITED GIFTS

You will use only a tiny fraction of what your PC offers, simply because a kindly feature of computer designers is their persistent wish to please everybody all the time in all circumstances. They insist, for instance, that you should be able to decide the vital issue of whether your Desktop should appear plain or stripy. (See **Start** – **Settings** – **Control Panel** – **Display**.)

You must learn to stand on your own two feet and make your own selections. You may, for instance, see on your Desktop these icons:

They're just empty Folders into which you can store Files or other Folders, in the usual way, by dragging or saving into them. You can make your own – right-click on the Desktop or on a window listing the names of Files or Folders, click New ▸ and ▨ Folder.

Exercise 22

EXTRAS AND SAFETY PRECAUTIONS

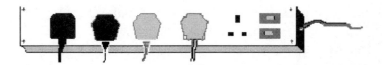

Ideally, there is interposed between your machine and mains electricity not just an **'anti-surge'** device but also an 'anti-peak' device, to protect against harmful variations in your local power supply. These devices are often incorporated in the sort of multi-socket strip used for plugging in several items. This safeguard is perhaps more necessary in the country than in cities, but is good insurance. As a further hazard, when your computer is plugged in, electricity from a thunderstorm miles away can damage it even if it's switched off, so unplug from the mains in stormy weather.

Unplug also, during thunderstorms or before you go on holiday, your printer from the mains and your modem from its telephone line. My local computer shop has today six melted modems and a damaged printer. You will see a wire from the back of your computer plugged in to a telephone socket in the wall. That wire comes from your modem.

One bit of maintenance you can do yourself is to **defragment**. Removing stuff from the Recycle Bin leaves untidy gaps in your machine which slows it down. Defragmentation from time to time is the answer. To do this Go Start – Programs ▶ Accessories ▶ System Tools ▶ Disk Defragmenter and follow the instructions. It may take quite a long time to run.

It might be useful for you to swap a 14 inch monitor for a larger one or to buy some more **RAM** (Random Access Memory), if your supplier says it will lessen the time that little hourglass ⧖ keeps you waiting. I had endless trouble with illegal operations and text going haywire when working on this book, until I discovered that my machine didn't have enough RAM to cope with the vast number of bytes needed for the numerous illustrations.

You might buy extras like a **scanner**, which can transfer pictures or text onto your screen for printing or modifying – removing red eye from a photograph for instance. There are also amazing games and other miraculous devices being invented as fast as anyone can think of them.

GOODBYE

Once Geraldine had stopped panicking, as she was instructed on the screen saver described on page 28, and had gone through the 22 exercises in this book, she was computer literate. She too can now word-process, manage documents, draw pictures, e-mail and web-surf with ease.

She will find that whatever equipment she buys is out-dated by the time her cheque is cashed or her credit card debited, but she can console herself with the thought that any new equipment which saves her a micro-second may take her macro-hours to master.

I wish you the very best of luck.

INDEX

This replaces a Glossary. To find the meaning of a word, look it up here. There's more explanation in the page referred to. On that page, the item referred to here is printed in **bold**, or is a sub-heading.

Plus sign on Windows Explorer, ⊞, 83.
Point, size of print, 49.
Pound sign £, 40.
Print Preview, 94.
Print Screen key, copies what shows on screen, ready for pasting later onto a File.
Printing in colour, 55; to start printing, 95.
Program: A set of instructions which tells your computer what to do.
Programs ▶, 30.

Q

Question mark: can be moved to a part of a window to explain it; on the Mouse Properties window, 19; explaining Match case in the Find window, 53.
Quick brown fox, 48.

R

RAM = Random Access Memory, 116.
Read only: a state of a File or disk when it can't be modified or written over. CD-ROMs are *read only*, ROM standing for **R**ead **O**nly **M**emory. Floppies can be made *read only* by pushing up the little tab at their top corner to open the hole. (Push down to close the hole and reverse this feature.) If you open a File and its Title declares, for no apparent reason, that it is *read only*, it may simply be that you have already opened it and it's quietly lurking on your Taskbar.
Receiving e-mail, 111.
Recycle Bin, 74; emptying, 75.
Register: when installing something, you're often asked to *register*. You don't have to. You don't have to give a salesperson your address.
Remove an item, such as Calculator, from the Start Menu, 80; remove highlighting, 44.
Rename a File or Folder, 73.
Replace a word in a File, 54.
Restore a deleted File, 75.
Reverse an Enter, 41.
Right-click on its button on the Taskbar to close a window, 26.
Right-clicks, 27; to Auto Arrange icons on Desktop, 81; to Cascade Windows, 26; to close a window from the Taskbar, 26; to make a new Folder, 62; to Move here or Copy here, 68, 78; to Minimise All Windows, 27; to make a shortcut to the Programs Folder on the Start Menu window, 80.
Ruler, tickable on or off on WordPad, 38; altering margins by dragging the blobs at each end of the ruler, 52.

then right-click it. This will produce a menu with **Properties** on it.
Click **Properties** and the Taskbar Properties window will appear.
Click the little square opposite **Always on top** until a tick remains
in the square. Click the little square opposite **Auto hide** until there
is no tick in it. Then click **OK**.